What the Effective Schools Research Says

Safe and Orderly Environment

Compiled by

Jo-Ann Cipriano Pepperl

Lawrence W. Lezotte

Published by:

Effective Schools Products, Ltd.
2199 Jolly Road, Suite 160
Okemos, Michigan 48864
(517) 349-8841 • FAX: (517) 349-8852
www.effectiveschools.com

What the Effective Schools Research Says:
Safe and Orderly Environment
Call for quantity discounts.

Manufactured and printed in the United States of America.

ISBN 1-883247-14-4

Dear Colleague:

What makes for a safe, orderly school environment?

Educators need the answer to this question today more than ever before. One of the best ways to focus the dialogue is to look at the research that has been conducted on general school climate and student behavior, physical plant of the school, student discipline, classroom management, and character education.

This document contains a compilation of over a decade of relevant school research on these topics. By studying what we have learned, we can make a real difference in the safety of our schools.

The first and second generation correlate on safe and orderly environment provides a good starting point:

The First Generation: In the effective school, there is an orderly, purposeful, businesslike atmosphere which is free from the threat of physical harm. The school climate is not oppressive and is conducive to teaching and learning.

The Second Generation: In the first generation, the safe and orderly environment correlate was defined in terms of the absence of undesirable student behavior (e.g., students fighting). In the second generation, the concept of a school environment conducive to **Learning for All** must move beyond the elimination of undesirable behavior. The second generation will place increased emphasis on the presence of certain desirable behaviors (e.g., cooperative team learning). These second generation schools will be places where students actually help one another.

Moving beyond simply the elimination of undesirable behavior will represent a significant challenge for many schools. For example, it is unlikely that a school's faculty could successfully teach its students to work together unless the adults in the school model collaborative behaviors in their own professional working relationships. Since schools as workplaces are characterized by their isolation, creating more collaborative/cooperative environments for both the adults and students will require substantial commitment and change in most schools.

First, teachers must learn the "technologies of teamwork." Second, the school will have to create the "opportunity structures" for collaboration. Finally, the staff will have to nurture the belief that collaboration, which often requires more time initially, will assist the schools to be more effective and satisfying in the long run.

But schools will not be able to get students to work together cooperatively unless they have been taught to respect human diversity and appreciate democratic values. These student learnings will require a major and sustained commitment to multicultural education. Students and the adults who teach them will need to come to terms with the fact that the United States is no longer a nation with minorities. We are now a nation of minorities. This new reality is currently being resisted by many of our community and parent advocacy groups, as well as by some educators.

The following research studies give us some guidance on how to achieve the goal of this all-important correlate of effective schools—a safe, secure learning environment for all. I hope it helps your school find the direction it needs to take.

Respectfully,

Lawrence W. Lezotte
Educational Consultant and Commentator

Table of Contents

Section II

Section III

Section IV

Section V

Section I

General School Climate

and Student Behavior

General School Climate and Student Behavior

People are the most important component of schools, and people tend to behave as they are treated. Misbehavior results, in part, because the school environment reinforces undesirable behaviors and fails to reinforce desirable ones.

Schools need to foster a positive, caring environment, where learning is valued and differences are accepted, to assure the development of each student's intellectual, social, emotional, and physical growth. Such an environment also reduces the possibility of school violence.

- Students benefit from support characterized by individual kindness and consideration. Likewise, teachers benefit from administrative support in dealing with discipline or in disputes with parents.

- Affiliation occurs when individuals feel connected to others around them. It is difficult to achieve this when the adults in a school are isolated from each other.

- The principal's belief that decision making should be shared has a critical impact on teacher commitment and school climate. Stable and consistent school environments appear strongest in schools where students and faculty participate in decision-making processes.

- The more principals can provide teachers with meaning and inspiration for their work, the stronger the organizational culture. The more teachers are enthusiastic about their work, the stronger the sharing of beliefs in the school.

- Students express a strong preference for working in groups, and clearly prefer a school where differences are valued rather than feared.

- Conflict management and mediation training empower students. Empowering students to regulate and control their own and their classmates' actions can decrease the amount of time and energy teachers and administrators spend on student conflicts.

- Orderly schools have a clear focus on appropriate student behavior, open communication about rules and regulations, formal discipline codes and classroom management plans, and expressed concern for students as individuals.

- Strategies for improving school climate and, thus, reducing or avoiding school violence include encouraging student participation in school governance, creating schools within schools, and engaging in activities that encourage greater involvement between students, parents, and the community.

- The safety and security of the school should be regularly assessed by students, staff, and the community. Also, student management issues must be analyzed through the use of objective data, collected over a period of time.

- Well-disciplined schools identify clear, concise, and relevant curriculum goals. Further, curriculum is seen as a living document, and is regularly evaluated and modified.

- Schools with an effective school climate put a strong emphasis on organizational variables, especially the attitudes, interests, and commitment of staff members.

- The greatest risk of student violence occurs during unstructured time when large numbers of students are interacting with one another.

- Programs listed as most effective in preventing violence include teachers present in hallways, stricter discipline policies, security personnel, peer mediation/conflict resolution training, and poverty issues programs.

- The adoption of school uniforms appears to be effective as a means of improving school climate and student behavior.

- In order to combat the unrelenting influence of media violence, schools must teach visual literacy in addition to print literacy. Children must be taught to critically evaluate the violence they see on screen.

- It is impossible to do the job alone. Schools must involve other resources such as police departments, courts, welfare organizations, etc.

In summary, the establishment of a caring school community is an important factor in a school's ability to make a difference in the lives of children. Making that connection can result in fewer disciplinary problems and a greater sense of pride, respect for others, and respect for self.

EFFECTIVE SCHOOLS RESEARCH ABSTRACTS

SAFE AND ORDERLY ENVIRONMENT

CITATION: Purkey, William W. and David N. Aspy, "The Mental Health of Students: Nobody Minds? Nobody Cares?" *Person-Centered Review* 3, 1 (February 1988): 41-49.

What Did the Researchers Do?

Having studied the outpouring of new programs, policies, mandates, edicts, and legislation calling for excellence in education, Purkey and Aspy note that educational reformers have almost universally neglected to address the affective/social development of students.

The researchers state with regret that none of the professional organizations in counseling or related fields have raised a clear voice of concern about the neglect of the emotional well-being of children. The journals and national conferences of these organizations have been caught up in this wave of "excellence."

In reaction to the several published reports in the '80's on the "ills" of education in our country, America went quickly to its schools and looked for weaknesses. Many critics felt that counseling services, affective programs, and social development courses were getting in the way of teaching the basics and were defined as the "frills" in education. Thus, affective education was linked to bad education, and concern for the mental health of students declined in our schools.

What Did the Researchers Find?

"Teacher behaviors which demean, humiliate, or deny the rights of students may be judged wrong despite any evidence that these behaviors promote desired outcomes—the end does not justify the means." (Rosenshine and McGaw, 1972) The researchers offer five axioms that may help balance our emphasis on academic achievement with concern for the mental health of children:

Schools that facilitate affective developments also facilitate cognitive development. Aspy and Roebuck (1977, 1985) explored the relationship between a facilitative climate and both self-concept and academic achievement. After analyzing 200,000 hours of classroom instruction, they concluded that classrooms that facilitated self-concept development also enhanced student achievement. Specifically, teachers who treat their students as able and respond to them empathetically promote cognitive and emotional growth. Conversely, teachers who do not do these things tend to retard growth in self-concept and in school achievement.

"Inviting" practices are related to positive outcomes. Educational practices based on self-concept theory reflect optimism, respect, and trust. They are intentionally inviting. In a series of studies, researchers reported a high correlation among inviting teacher practices, identified by Amos (1985) as consideration, commitment, coordination, proficiency, and expectation, and student affective outcomes, such as attitudes toward course subject matter, instructor, and self-as-learner.

Students learn more when they see themselves as able, valuable, and responsible. Recent brain research provides information that supports the need for emotionally healthy classrooms. When students are placed in environments where they begin to doubt their own value, abilities, or self-directing powers, it appears that the brain physically represses information that is threatening to the perceived self. The vast literature on self-concept would also support this brain research, since it generally concludes that people tend to behave as they are treated.

Students learn more when they choose to learn. Academic achievement is most likely to occur when both teachers and students see the educative process as a cooperative effort in which students want to learn. The important assumption here is that the conditions in the environment support students wanting to be successful learners.

People are the most important component of schools. Billions of dollars have been spent on the cognitive components of education, but we have spent next to nothing on creating positive emotional environments in schools. The mental health of our children and adults in our schools and their feelings of self-worth and self-efficacy should be of utmost importance.

What Are Possible Implications for School Improvement?

Effective schools research-based school improvement stresses the importance of school (or school-district) climate. Schools should foster a positive, caring environment, where learning is valued and differences are accepted, so as to assure the development of each student's intellectual, social, emotional, and physical growth.

The following effective schools beliefs support the five axioms offered in this article:

- All students can learn.

- There are no unimportant adults or children in school.

- Teachers, administrators, and students are already doing the best they know how to do, given the conditions in which they find themselves.

- People want to succeed.

- Teachers cause learning.

Two characteristics of effective schools refer directly to the importance of a positive school climate. A Safe and Orderly Environment dispels the threat of physical harm, producing a school climate that is supportive and is conducive to teaching and learning. High Expectations for Success describes an effective school in which the staff believes and demonstrates that all students can attain mastery of the essential school skills and that they, the staff, can help all students attain mastery.

The effective schools model also specifically addresses the issue of dollars invested in the "renewal" process as a vital part of staff development. Schools in our nation spend on an average less than two percent on the renewal and upgrading of their human resources. We need to increase over time the amount of money we invest in people in our schools. This renewal effort must include attention to the social and emotional growth of both adults and children. We know that, when teachers have feelings of efficacy, it influences how their students feel about themselves.

— Michelle Maksimowicz

SAFE AND ORDERLY ENVIRONMENT

CITATION: Firestone, William A. and Sheila Rosenblum, "Building Commitment in Urban High Schools," *Educational Evaluation and Policy Analysis* 10, 4 (Winter 1988): 285-299.

What Did the Researchers Do?

Urban comprehensive high schools face a series of related problems—poor attendance, high dropout rates, low achievement, poor relationships among ethnic groups, and teacher burnout resulting in reduced commitment and high turnover. Policymakers generally focus on problems in a piecemeal way without recognizing their relatedness. But the researchers see an underlying issue linking these problems—that of commitment. They contend that student and teacher commitment typically are treated separately, but that "teachers and students spend so much time together that the orientations of each influence those of the other and...the orientations of both groups are strongly influenced by some of the same school factors."[1]

On behalf of superintendents from five urban school systems—Baltimore, Newark, Philadelphia, Pittsburgh, and Washington, D.C.—the researchers launched a study to examine the commitment issue. Two comprehensive inner-city high schools from each of the five districts were selected for study. The paired schools had similar student bodies, but, in each pair, one reflected the most difficult problems of these schools. Schools ranged in size from less than 1,100 to more than 2,500. In seven schools, three-fourths or more of the students were black. In eight schools, two-fifths or more received a free lunch. In six schools, daily attendance was low, ranging from 72 to 85 percent.

Data about these schools were collected in the district office and through on-site interviews. The interviews were conducted with administrative staff, counselors, and a cross section of both teachers and students.

What Did the Researchers Find?

As a result of the study, a framework was developed that illustrates the dynamics of teacher and student commitment and how school administrators and district policymakers can influence these by promoting certain school factors. Specifically, in answer to the question, "Commitment to what?", three dimensions of teacher commitment and two dimensions of student commitment were identified. Teacher commitments were to students: "I stay because of the feedback I get from the students I helped." To teaching: "A good day is when the students learn. When you test and everyone does well." To the specific place: "I was offered a permanent slot at another school, but I stayed here...I'm ready to try something different, but I want to do it here."

Student commitments were to learning: "A good day is when you understand the classwork and you know something new at the end of the day." To place: "School is important because it is where a student can come to be with friends."

Researchers also found that each of the teacher dimensions (commitment to students, teaching, and place), provides the basis for certain teacher behaviors. Each behavior is positive in itself, but will only produce an overall desired effect in combination with other positive behaviors. For example, "commitment to place is associated with considerable loyalty to the school. Its manifestations include continued tenure and willingness to take on a variety of roles, but it does not have implications for how teaching will be carried out." (p. 288)

Furthermore, researchers found that teachers and students can create a mutually reinforcing cycle that reduces or enhances overall commitment within the school. Students want teachers who exhibit a certain level of respect for them, which is reflected in what teachers say, how they act, and how they use time. Similarly, teachers' commitment to their work is, to a great extent, derived from the response they get from students.

Two factors may contribute negatively to this dynamic. "The first is externalization of responsibility. To preserve their professional self-respect, some teachers blame their students' low achievement on their family backgrounds and blame failure to implement new district initiatives on lack of firm building leadership. By shifting responsibility to some others, teachers justify their continuation in patterns of behavior that are no longer functional for the current situation." (p. 289) The second factor related to commitment level is student behavior. "Teachers are worn down by disruptive behaviors in the classroom and in the corridors...They become lethargic or impatient, stop explaining things to students, and in extreme cases become verbally abusive. These behaviors in turn depress student commitment still further." (p. 290)

This study also identifies five factors that affect how these cycles of commitment are played out in the school. Schools with higher levels of commitment demonstrated greater success with these factors:

Relevance. Relevance stems from a sense of purpose in one's work. It is difficult to achieve this in comprehensive high schools because they tend to be organizations "in which everything is available" and where classroom activities relate very little to the difficult daily situations that urban students face.

Respect and affiliation. Affiliation occurs when individuals feel connected to others in their surroundings; yet the organization of the high school does little to promote this. Teachers are isolated from peers and administrators. Students feel that teachers blame them for educational problems. Treating low achievement as a problem to be solved can help this situation, as can increasing the interactions among adults in the school.

Support. Administrative support for teachers contributes to their performance and willingness to stay in the field. Such things as reduced paper work, dealing with discipline, and support in disputes with parents are examples of the kind of support that teachers want. Similar factors relate to student support. If barriers to learning (like discipline) are removed, students are more likely to succeed. Students also benefit from support characterized by individual kindness and consideration.

Expectations. When individuals become committed to a performance objective, they will strive to attain it. Likewise, they will accomplish less when no expectation is set. When a teacher has higher expectations for students, the students accomplish more. When a principal holds high expectations for teachers, the teachers will respond in the same way.

Influence. Individuals are most highly committed to jobs that give them autonomy and discretion. Providing opportunities for teacher influence has a substantial impact on teacher commitment. Teachers value autonomy in the classroom and want influence over day-to-day decisions that affect them. A variety of formal arrangements for shared decision making may exist within the school, but most crucial is the principal's belief that the process should be shared with teachers.

What Are Possible Implications for School Improvement?

This examination of commitment in urban high schools points out that there are a number of dimensions of commitment that need to be addressed. The authors suggest that a vicious "self-fulfilling" cycle can operate, with teacher alienation contributing to student alienation and vice versa. The study identifies school-wide factors that may be addressed to break this cycle. These findings substantiate the importance of a comprehensive model for school improvement, rather than a "single project" approach. Levels of commitment in schools are tied to overall cultural norms, beliefs, and attitudes. Thus, school improvement needs to be thought of as cultural change. The five school commitment dimensions explored in this study provide a framework for evaluating existing cultural norms and for developing improvement plans. Additionally, the close relationship between teacher and student attitudes in the study may indicate the need to evaluate the role of high school students in school improvement activities.

— Lydia L. McCue

[1] Dworkin, A.G., *Teacher Burnout in the Public Schools: Structural Causes and Consequences for Children*. Albany, NY, SUNY Press, 1987, quoted by Firestone and Rosenblum, p. 286.

EFFECTIVE SCHOOLS RESEARCH ABSTRACTS

SAFE AND ORDERLY ENVIRONMENT

CITATION: Davis, Gary A., and Margaret A. Thomas, *Effective Schools and Effective Teachers*. Allyn and Bacon, Boston, MA, 1989.

What Did the Researchers Do?

This book was written for classroom teachers and administrators to provide an introduction to the major findings of effective schools research. It focuses on the characteristics of schools that are related to higher levels of student achievement, traits of principals who contribute to school success, and teacher characteristics and classroom behaviors that produce high achievement. The book is heavily documented with relevant research incorporated in a meaningful and understandable approach for the educational practitioner.

What Did the Researchers Find?

The book is organized around four main topics, supplemented by a discussion of the principal-teacher observation and supervision process and strategies for teacher collaboration to improve teaching.

Characteristics of effective schools. A number of researchers have identified characteristics of effective schools. While all of the lists cited by the authors are not identical, they do correlate well with those identified by Ron Edmonds. He stated: "What effective schools share is a climate in which it is incumbent on all personnel to be instructionally effective for all pupils."[1] Yet there is no one plan that a school can follow that will lead to effectiveness. Schools differ in the composition of their student body and groupings, resulting in differing needs and problems of students; community values and expectations; internal school climate; staff organization; and strengths. Therefore, the principal and faculty must adapt the research and planning strategies to their own needs and the needs of their school in order to create an optimal improvement plan.

Characteristics of effective principals. Citing Fred Hechinger's comment that he has "never seen a good school with a poor principal or a poor school with a good principal," the authors discuss the qualities and behaviors that characterize principals in successful schools.[2] While there is no one ideal leadership style, effective principals focus on leadership that develops a productive and satisfying work environment for teachers and promotes growth in student learning. The principal's vision serves as a guide for the faculty when setting goals and objectives, assessing how well the school is functioning, and setting academic and behavioral expectations for students—in short, the academic, instructional, and social climate for the students and staff within a school building. Faculty empowerment in the school improvement process remains critical, but many researchers believe that strong instructional leadership by a principal with vision is the single most critical component of a successful, effective school.

"Good instructional leaders also monitor teaching progress by observing their teachers at work in the classroom and providing feedback after every observation...teachers are praised for good work and positive contributions. When teaching problems arise, these principals provide supportive assistance that produces improvement." (p. 29)

Characteristics of effective teachers. While the statistical correlations between teaching variables and achievement are low, the authors point out that even weak relationships can make a difference in student learning. Many small improvements in teaching can add up to positive changes in student achievement. Teachers involved in school improvement and training directed at increasing teacher effectiveness are almost certain to make a difference in student achievement. Of all the variables contributing to student achievement, research has confirmed that the most crucial factor is academic engagement, or time on task.

Effective classroom management. Considered essential for good achievement, behavior, and attitudes, good classroom management aims at increasing time on task and reducing disruptions. It is largely preventative and is achieved by establishing positive expectations, clear rules, communication to the students that the teacher knows what is going on in the classroom, classroom organization and activities, and responses to misbehavior. Teachers must have the ability to handle two classroom matters at once; especially, they must be able to handle deviancy without disrupting the current learning activity.

These four topics are not isolated, but rather interrelate and overlap. They are most enhanced when combined with an approach to supervision that includes peer observation and coaching and administrative supervision focusing on the principles of effective schooling, effective teaching, classroom management, and professional responsibilities. For this to happen most productively, the principal must create an atmosphere within the building that is collegial in nature, emphasizing teacher strengths. This allows teachers to feel secure enough to analyze and explore ways to improve their effectiveness. Teachers working together provide "an expanded pool of ideas, materials, and methods and a collective ability to generate higher-quality solutions to problems." (Little, 1987, cited p. 175)

Peer observation and coaching can be more effective in promoting change and improvement than hierarchical supervision by an administrator. Yet, such supervision is a necessary part of the educational arena. A principal will be able to effect change and improvement in teaching when the atmosphere is conducive to open and meaningful dialogue between administrator and teacher.

What Are Possible Implications for School Improvement?

Educators embarking on or involved in school improvement must obtain knowledge of the carefully identified and confirmed principles surrounding effective schools and effective teaching. The four topics presented in this book, combined with peer and administrator observation and coaching, provide a good outline for improving school and teacher effectiveness. The material is presented in a format that is meaningful and practical for teachers and administrators while incorporating research in a viable manner. The authors do a good job of illustrating the interrelatedness of the topics presented, which should help school faculty members see the importance of a well-thought-out approach focusing on the most important variables for their particular school situation.

— Lee Gerard

[1] Edmonds, Ronald R., "Effective Schools for the Urban Poor," *Educational Leadership* 37, 2 (October 1979): 15–27.

[2] Introduction to Lipham, J. M., *Effective Principal, Effective School*. National Association of Secondary School Principals, Reston, VA, 1981.

EFFECTIVE SCHOOLS RESEARCH ABSTRACTS

SAFE AND ORDERLY ENVIRONMENT

CITATION: Deal, Terrence E. and Kent D. Peterson, *The Principal's Role in Shaping School Culture*. Office of Educational Research and Improvement, U.S. Department of Education, Washington, D.C., 1990.

What Did the Researchers Do?

As national goals are set for schools in the '90s—high school completion, increased student achievement, increased performance in science and mathematics, and safe, disciplined, drug-free schools—principals increasingly will need more authority and responsibility for reforming their schools. But "success is unlikely unless reforms are linked meaningfully to the daily realities and deep structure of life in schools. This is more apt to occur when principals understand and reckon with the power of school culture," say Deal and Peterson. This monograph was written "to explain—and give examples—of how principals can shape the culture of schools." (p. 1)

Deal and Peterson describe how current school reform has influenced the operations of schools, linking the success of school reform to the concepts of school culture and symbolic leadership. The researchers illustrate their proposition with case studies of school leaders in five different schools that had been successful in reshaping their school's culture.

What Did the Researchers Find?

Deal and Peterson point out that different reform strategies used by instructional leaders reflect their assumptions about how schools and people work. Four basic school reform approaches were identified:

- The human resources approach emphasizes the skills and needs of those who work in the school. This strategy focuses on teacher selection and training, staff development, and administrative inservice.

- The structural approach focuses on goals, roles, coordination, and control. This approach assumes people work best when there is a clear focus for the school. Procedures and routines are set to allow work to proceed efficiently.

- The political approach rests upon power, conflict, bargaining, and coalitions. This approach "assumes that good school functioning depends on forming working coalitions around school purposes and practices." (p. 5)

- The economic approach assumes principals and teachers will work harder to supply good service and services tailored to local needs if schools are placed in competition by allowing parents and students to select which school to attend.

Deal and Peterson argue that school leaders, teachers, parents, and students need to consider a fifth strategy—one that is tied to the concept of school culture. "While recognizing the powerful ways in which these other approaches operate, the concept of culture underlies and helps connect each of the other four." (p. 4)

School culture is built on those values, beliefs, and traditions which shape the behaviors of the members of the school community; it is evident in talking with teachers, parents, and students. Deal and Peterson point out that research both in effective schools and top performing companies indicate that productivity is linked to the culture of the organization, be it a school or a company. Successful schools have:

- strong values that support a safe and secure environment that is conducive to learning;

- high expectations for every student and faculty member;

- a belief in the importance of basic skill mastery for every student, holding this as a critical goal;

- clear performance standards and the belief that all students and faculty members should receive feedback which is clear and helpful;

- a high regard for strong leadership.

The five different schools in the case studies presented by the researchers represent public and private; elementary and secondary; affluent and poor; urban, suburban, and rural. But, in all five schools, the researchers found common tactics used by each principal:

- developing a strong sense of what the school should be;

- selecting staff whose values fit well with the values of the principal and school;

- facing conflict and building school unity through the resolution of disputes;

- using his/her own behavior and actions to exemplify core values and beliefs, and reinforcing those values and beliefs through daily routines;

- telling stories that reinforce and exemplify shared values;

- caring for and continuing those traditions, ceremonies, rituals, and symbols that reflect and reinforce the school's culture. (p. 80)

What Are Possible Implications for School Improvement?

Lasting school change is complex and takes time. Effective schools do not happen overnight or at the end of one school year. Effective schools—schools where student outcomes are not dependent upon gender, ethnicity, or socioeconomic status—take strong leadership that has a clear and well-articulated vision. The changes wrought by a principal who reshapes those aspects of a school culture in order to improve positive outcomes will indeed outlast simple program changes. Many school improvement efforts are based upon a given program. But when these programs are implemented, the values, beliefs, and norms of the school are overlooked, and the program fails.

Any successful reform effort must be congruent with the school's culture. An excellent suggestion made by Deal and Peterson is to have the school faculty discuss the history of the school. Through such a discussion, the faculty can identify the school's values, beliefs, and traditions. Such a strategy will enable the faculty to see those aspects of the school's culture that need to be changed and those that need to be strengthened.

A principal who understands how school culture (values, norms, and beliefs) influences a school enjoys a great advantage. Such knowledge allows the principal to take actions which will help the school improve and avoid situations which may lead to negative repercussions. There's more to a principal's role than managing schedules, buses, and budgets. The principal is constantly watched by the students, teachers, and parents. What he or she says, attends to, or appreciates will have an impact on the school's culture.

The researchers emphasize that "one of the most significant roles of leaders (and of leadership) is the creation, encouragement, and refinement of the symbols and symbolic activity that give meaning to the organization...the effectiveness of a leader is in the ability to make actions meaningful to others." (p. 13)

— J. Mark Lubbers

EFFECTIVE SCHOOLS RESEARCH ABSTRACTS

SAFE AND ORDERLY ENVIRONMENT

CITATION: Werthamer-Larsson, Lisa, et al., "Effect of First-Grade Classroom Environment on Shy Behavior, Aggressive Behavior, and Concentration Problems," *American Journal of Community Psychology* 19, 4 (August 1991): 585-602.

What Did the Researchers Do?

Do classroom achievement and behavior environments predict child behavior? This is the question that the researchers sought to answer in this study, noting that there has been little previous research on this question. "The social learning theory proposition that children learn by observing others, especially multiple peer models (Bandura, 1986, Schunk, Hanson & Cox, 1987),[1] leads us to hypothesize that low-achieving classroom environments and poor-behaving classroom environments will lead to child behavior problems." (p. 587) Social learning theory also led the researchers to hypothesize that children who are repeating a grade will have higher rates of behavior problems in the classroom if it is a low-achieving or poor-behaving classroom.

Previous research has dealt primarily with child behavior problems related to the characteristics of the family environment, the classroom role in socialization, classroom instructional and management strategies, and ability grouping as predictors of achievement. The research forming the basis for this article was conducted at the first-grade level because of the importance of first grade to the child's successful transition to school. First-grade behavior and symptoms are also predictive of late adolescent and early adult outcomes. Behavior problems were identified as shy behavior, disobedience and aggressive behavior, and poor concentration.

The population for this study was first-grade children attending Baltimore City Public Schools in East Baltimore. This large urban area was chosen because it represented a varied socioeconomic and racial mixture which ranged from predominantly African-American, low-income areas to a predominantly white, moderate-income area. The sample consisted of 609 children in 26 first-grade classrooms.

What Did the Researchers Find?

Their analysis of the data clearly showed that the classroom achievement environment contributes to children's shy behavior and aggressive behavior. The classroom behavior environment also contributes to children's shy behavior. The researchers had analyzed the data to control for the possible effect of child characteristics significantly related to child behavior, such as gender, age, kindergarten work habit problems, repeater, preschool experience, and between-year change.

The classroom behavior environment had an impact on students who had repeated a grade, compared with nonrepeaters in terms of aggressive behavior. Classroom achievement environment affected the shy behavior of repeaters compared to nonrepeaters. Combined, these results further support previous findings that low-achieving and poor-behaving classroom environments have a negative impact on a child's behavior.

These results also suggest that the achievement and behavior characteristics of a classroom affect child behavior in different ways. For example, low achievement and disruptive classrooms both had negative influences on children playing with other children. On the other hand, only low classroom achievement showed increased incidents of breaking rules, yelling, breaking things, and fighting. Neither low-achieving nor poor-behaving classroom environments increased the incidence on children working well alone, completing assignments, and paying attention.

Considerable thought has been given to potential explanations of the effect of low-achieving classrooms and poor-behaving classrooms on child behavior. Low-achieving and misbehaving classrooms quickly attain the reputation of being "at-risk classrooms," labeling the children in them as opposed to labeling the environment. As a result, these children are stigmatized; they develop low self-esteem, lose motivation, and begin to perform poorly. Another possibility is that children in these classrooms model poor behavior. A third possibility is that teachers of these kinds of classrooms alter the pace and quality of instruction. Such instructional strategies could indirectly influence child behavior. There is evidence that the quality of children's peer relationships in first grade predicts adjustment problems in adolescence. Low-achieving and poor-behaving classrooms may foster peer rejection, which may, in turn, lead to feelings of loneliness and incompetence.

The impact of low-achieving and poor-behaving classrooms on repeaters could be explained similarly. Repeaters may be more likely than nonrepeaters to be labeled by their teachers and peers. Children who have already experienced failure may be more likely to model the performance of their peers than children who have not.

Teachers who perceive classes with at-risk students as "bad" may have a more difficult time managing such classes. Students whom these teachers consider to be at risk will, in turn, be more likely to behave inappropriately when they receive less teacher attention than other children in the class.

Teachers may spend more of their time interacting with high-achieving students than with low-achieving students. It is possible that repeaters may be more likely to be rejected than nonrepeaters.

What Are Possible Implications for School Improvement?

These results support the importance of effective classroom management in terms of behavior and achievement. One of the major considerations for schools, as a result of this and related research, should be to design interventions that reduce classroom misbehavior and learning problems. Assistance for teachers in strategies which deal effectively with difficult students and low-achieving students would be an important component to build into district or building resources. If classroom environment independently contributes to behavior, as these results suggest, the modification of school tracking or strict ability-grouping practices would be an important focus for school improvement teams. This research, combined with other research on the detrimental effect of tracking, provides school improvement teams and administrators with a strong rationale for developing alternatives to improve the potential for all students to succeed.

— Lee Gerard

[1] Bandura, A., *Social Foundations of Thought and Action: A Social Cognitive Theory*. Prentice-Hall, Englewood Cliffs, NJ, 1986. Schunk, O.H., A.R. Hanson, and P.D. Cox, "Peer Model Attributes and Children's Achievement Behaviors," *Journal of Educational Psychology* 79, pp. 54–61.

CITATION: Thompson, Scott, "School Culture in Transformation," *Equity and Choice* 3, 1 (Fall 1991): 19-24.

What Did the Researcher Do?

Case studies of individual effective schools are rare. Well-written descriptions are even more rare. But this article presents an excellent portrait of the Samuel Gompers Fine Arts Option School (Grades 4–8) on the far south side of Chicago. To qualify as an option school, Gompers had to serve a racially isolated, high poverty-index population. (An option school should not be confused with a magnet school.)

What Did the Researcher Find?

Built in 1929, the school originally served a mostly white community. During the 1970's, it became an all-black school in a predominantly black community. For more than 15 years, Gompers was "a tough place—dangerous and unpredictable," according to one teacher's description. (p. 20) Gangs came to school with weapons and failed to keep their distance. Attendance and test scores were down. The building was dilapidated, and parents did not want to send their children to it.

In the fall of 1984 when a new principal was needed, the school's local advisory council appointed a committee of parents and teachers to participate in the selection process. The committee screened candidates, interviewed them, and conducted follow-up interviews. Ultimately, they submitted recommendations to the General Superintendent who made the final selection. "This process gave the school and the community a sense of ownership, even though the final decision was out of their hands." (p. 22) When Blondean Y. Davis came to the school, she came "with a vision—that the school's prosperity depends on a spirit of high expectations and a focus for excellence." (p. 20) She developed a two-pronged approach for turning the school around. The first was to eliminate security concerns so that there would be no fear either in the school or on the grounds which the

school controls. This was solved by "cracking down." If someone was in school who was not supposed to be there, he or she was arrested. Consequently, Principal Davis was frequently in court. In addition, the school developed a "code yellow." When there were warnings of gang activity, the faculty and staff would stand around the school. The last "code yellow" occurred about three years ago. Davis' emphasis on security enabled the school to fulfill her dream of it being "a sanctuary for teachers and children." (p. 20)

Last year, for the first time, students were expected to wear uniforms. This helped to improve the discipline atmosphere and ease rivalry over clothes. Further, uniforms eliminated the problem of leather jackets and similar articles being stolen from children on the way to and from school. In some of the classes, teachers also wore the uniform. Nearly all students wear the uniform, but a few come from homes that do not support the idea.

The second prong of Davis' two-pronged approach to put the school on the road to excellence was to invest in a specific program so that there would be a model of excellence within the school. She felt that it had to be a program which would respond quickly and chose the music program because of the quality of the teacher in charge and because of the students' interest in music. A band and a chorus were formed. Participation in them became a privilege, and students lost this privilege by not maintaining a certain academic or social standing. The music teachers secured many public engagements for the band and chorus in Chicago and beyond. This was a motivation for students in the chorus and band, and it increased overall student pride in the school.

The improved security and the new chorus and band enabled the school to do something it had not done for many years: open its doors to the community for a nighttime event. An annual Fine Arts Festival was organized, with 400 parents and citizens attending the first year and many more in recent years. The festival "says what we're all about," Davis observes, "One of the things that's very important that people have to realize is that, if they do not have faith and participate in the community school and encourage the school to improve its standards, then basically they're lost." (p. 21)

Community involvement is encouraged in other ways, too. During Parent Booster Week, parents attend classes with their children for half a day. Parent and community volunteers serve in classrooms and are the source of paid Chapter 1 teaching assistants. Parent Partnership meetings are held in the evening and are open to the "entire 'Gompers family': children, parents, teachers and other members of the community." (p. 23) Student awards "are not serendipitous perks as at many other schools; they are a steady, integral force in the school's redefining of itself." (p. 20) Pennants are given out quarterly for perfect attendance. Honor roll students are recognized; so is each chorus and band member. An eighth grade awards luncheon is held at the Holiday Inn where virtually every eighth grader is recognized for something. And, there is an awards assembly for all the other students in the school.

Other programs have been installed to improve the quality of the educational program. All students take visual arts and Spanish classes—options which most Chicago elementary schools are unable to offer. Other new programs are DEAR (Drop Everything And Read), Academic Olympics, frequent field trips, a partnership with Chicago State University in science and math, and a Jostens integrated learning computer laboratory.

It's daunting to see what's required to achieve what Gompers has achieved. The author believes much of that achievement must be credited to Davis' willingness to put in 12- to 14-hour days coordinating and leading programs, activities, and resources.

The work of an educational leader is "not all about test scores," Davis says. "It's about many, many intangible things, and things that children take home and tell their parents." (p. 23)

What Are Possible Implications for School Improvement?

The recent history of Samuel Gompers Fine Arts Option School is living evidence that with hard work and inspired vision a school's culture can be radically transformed. Thompson's short, well-written article should be reproduced in its entirety and given to teachers and administrators embarking upon an effective schools project. The opportunity to visit or read about effective inner-city schools can make a critical difference to teachers and principals embarking on an effective schools project, as Rufus Young discovered when he guided the formation of an effective schools program in the St. Louis Public Schools. [1]

Thompson's article shows that it is possible to take a school which is "on the ropes" and turn it into a good school. And although the author did not refer to the effective schools correlates, he paints a word picture of many of them as he describes the school.

- Instructional Leadership—The vision and work of the new principal.

- High Expectations for Success and Clear School Mission—The principal's vision "that the school's prosperity depends on a spirit of high expectations and a focus on excellence." (p. 20) Shaping the student awards program to the mission of the school.

- Safe and Orderly Environment—The emphasis on security in the building and on school grounds.

- Home-School Relations—The Fine Arts Festival, Parent Booster Week, parent and citizen volunteers in the classrooms, etc.

- Opportunity to Learn—The installation of new programs such as band, chorus, visual arts and Spanish classes for all, Academic Olympics, DEAR (Drop Everything And Read), etc.

Summing it all up is Thompson's statement at the beginning of his article, which should be thoughtfully, and fully discussed by all: "A school is not really a building. A school, of course, is people and ideas in action. It's what students and instructors and administrators accomplish together. (p. 19)

— Robert E. Sudlow

---

[1] See Young, Rufus, "A Process for Developing More Effective Urban Schools: A Case Study of Stowe Middle School," *The Journal of Negro Education* 57, 3 (Summer 1988): 307–334. (*Effective Schools Research Abstracts*, Vol. 3, No. 4.)

EFFECTIVE SCHOOLS RESEARCH ABSTRACTS

SAFE AND ORDERLY ENVIRONMENT

CITATION: Phelan, Patricia, Ann Locke Davidson, and Hanh Thanh Cao, "Speaking Up: Students' Perspectives on School," *Phi Delta Kappan* 73, 9 (May 1992): 695-704.

What Did the Researchers Do?

This study should be required reading for all teachers and administrators—those currently working in schools and colleges, as well as those in preservice! It reveals that high school students have a great deal to say about school and classroom conditions that influence what they do, how they feel about themselves, and how they perceive their school as a workplace. The congruence between students' perceptions and those of teachers are remarkably similar!

In an effort to understand the nature of high school environments that support and foster positive learning experiences, the researchers interviewed students in two California school districts who were in their first year of high school, and the study followed them for two years. (p. 696) Data were collected through the use of interviews, classroom observations, and analysis of student records.

What Did the Researchers Find?

Students want what teachers want! Students from all achievement levels and sociocultural backgrounds want to succeed and want to be in an environment where it is possible for them to do so. Students' perceptions match not only the perceptions of educators, but also "match remarkably well those of contemporary theorists concerned with learning theory, cognitive science, and the sociology of work." (p. 696) Student perceptions were reported in seven categories discussed below.

Classroom environments. Students say they like classrooms where they feel they know the teacher and the other students. They want teachers to recognize who they are, to listen to what they have to say, and to respect their efforts. Their desire for a personal element in the classroom may suggest why the majority of students prefer to be in classes with friends. They claim that "having classmates whom

they know, trust, and can depend on for help is extremely important." (p. 696) In fact, some students say that the more friends they have in a class, the more involved they are with it.

Emotional safety is another important factor in classroom climate. Students do not like to be put down or made to "feel stupid, either by the teacher or by their peers." (p. 698) As one student expressed it, "I don't like teachers that go 'No, we explained it once and that's it.'" (p. 698)

Relationships with teachers. Students want teachers who care. This desire for caring teachers was such a pervasive response that the researchers have projected that "it speaks to the quiet desperation and loneliness of many adolescents in today's society." (p. 698) There are some differences in the ways high- and low-achieving students define caring behavior. High-achievers often associate caring with assistance in academic matters, like taking the time to read and critique a paper and to write comments. However, these students generally receive high grades regardless of their feelings about teachers. Working toward internalized goals seems to take precedence over any immediate discomfort they feel in a particular class. Low-achieving students often equate caring with certain personality traits (humor, patience, ability to listen) and a willingness to give person-to-person assistance on academic matters. These students frequently express their preference for this direct and personal attention that extends beyond assistance with school work. Their perceptions of teachers as caring or not appear to have direct consequences. If a teacher is viewed as not caring, students report a lack of incentive to do classwork or to participate in that teacher's class. On the other hand "caring teachers may be in a pivotal position to influence students who are teetering between involvement in school and withdrawal." (p. 699) In general, all students categorize teachers as those who like students and like to teach and those who don't. Humor, openness, and consideration help connect students with their teachers.

Pedagogy. "Perhaps the most resounding theme in discussions with students about pedagogy is that they want to learn from teachers, rather than simply read textbooks." (p. 699) Students seem unanimous in their dislike of reading textbook chapters and answering only the end-of-chapter questions. Students are quick to distinguish between teachers who talk with them and those who talk at them. Thus, the teachers who depend primarily on the lecture method of instruction risk alienating many students.

Both high- and low-achieving students prefer teachers who engage them in the learning process by holding discussions in which ideas are explored and shared. Students praise teachers who demonstrate respect for their ideas and opinions. In order to enable students to participate in class and to do so without fear, "it is crucial that teachers model and promote norms of interaction that ensure consideration and respect for all individuals." (p. 700) When a variety of teaching methods are used, students report a high level of interest. Students expressed a preference for teachers who are willing and able to assist them in understanding the material, and who take time to help them learn. Time after time, students tell of their frustrations in trying to understand course material and the failure of teachers to help them.

Both high- and low-achieving students expressed a strong preference for working in groups. High-ability students sometimes feel exploited in mixed-ability groups, saying they end up doing their own work and that of less-motivated students. But, when all students in these groups have been trained in cooperative techniques, both high- and low-level students report a high level of involvement and enjoyment.

School environments. Students are particularly sensitive to school climate. They attach great importance to the collective message conveyed by the attitudes of the faculty and administration about the "meaning of school and the importance of being there." (p. 702) One student compared her present school to one she had previously attended: "And then I got here and the teachers that I met, the first day they had my name right...I was tardy to class once, a couple of minutes late, and that day they called my house to talk to my parents...you're not there for a day and they notice and they...care." (p. 702)

Intergroup relationships. Perhaps the most important aspect of school climate for students is the level of tension or ease underlying peer interactions. They may learn to adjust to meanness in the environment, but they clearly prefer a school where "differences are valued rather than feared." (p. 702)

Group boundaries and behaviors. In almost all schools, students segregate themselves primarily by ethnicity and social class. However, in some schools, boundaries are fluid and students move between groups with ease. When group boundaries are rigid, students are less inclined to work cooperatively with those different from themselves. "The quality of intergroup relationships also affects students' interactions in classrooms." (p. 703) If there is tension between or within groups, energy can be diverted from academics. The researchers suggest that efforts in cooperative learning or detracking be undertaken only when the school climate, including intergroup relationships, is clearly understood from the students' perspective.

Student behaviors. For the most part, students dislike disruptive behaviors by other students. They desire an atmosphere in which people's actions are predictable, and adults negotiate acceptable norms of behaviors with students. This desire for reasonable behavior by their peers is almost always related to the need to feel safe and comfortable in school environments. Students feel angry at a system that they perceive as caring little about their actions.

What Are Possible Implications for School Improvement?

Both students and teachers want to be respected; work with others who care; exhibit humor, openness, and consideration; be actively involved in the learning process; and work in safe and tension-free environments. Aren't these attributes remarkably similar to the correlates of effective schools? How many staffs utilize these mutual desires when planning school improvement activities and strategies? Too often the plans written by staff (with few or no students involved) seem to focus on what the students "need to have done to them" rather than the congruence of mutual needs and desires. "Such miscommunication can lead to a perception of students as adversaries to be managed, rather than as individuals to be engaged as co-conspirators in creating optimal learning situations." (p. 704)

— Barbara C. Jacoby

EFFECTIVE SCHOOLS RESEARCH ABSTRACTS

SAFE AND ORDERLY ENVIRONMENT

CITATION: Johnson, David W., Roger T. Johnson, Bruce Dudley, and Robert Burnett, "Teaching Students to be Peer Mediators," *Educational Leadership* 50, 1 (September 1992): 10-13.

What Did the Researchers Do?

Do teachers and principals spend too much time resolving student conflicts—time which could be devoted to instruction and other activities central to the mission of the schools? Should traditional disciplinary procedures be re-examined and revised, since they have not proved effective in reducing the number of conflicts in the school? The authors of this article view discipline procedures on a continuum, with one end representing the use of external rewards and punishments, and the other end, self-regulation. Traditional discipline programs require an adult to monitor student behavior, determine whether it is acceptable or unacceptable, force students to cease inappropriate actions, and then impose punishment that is often unrelated to the offense.

The Peacemaker Program described in this article is an effort to teach students self-responsibility and self-regulation. To regulate their own behavior, students must be able to monitor their actions, assess the situation, make judgments as to which behaviors are appropriate, and change how they behave in order to act in an acceptable and desirable way. The article describes the situation in a typical school in which students are involved in conflicts with each other daily, including teasing and put-downs, playground conflicts, physical aggression or fights, access or possession conflicts, and turn-taking conflicts. Before the Peacemaker Program was implemented, such conflicts were normally taken to the teacher for resolution, or the students would use destructive strategies which would tend to escalate the conflict rather than resolving it.

The researchers report on their two-year experience with the Peacemaker Program, which they implemented in the Highlands Elementary School, a suburban middle-class school in Edina, Minnesota.

Students received 30 minutes of instruction and training per day for 30 days. They learned the principles and skills of negotiation and mediation, which, as "peacemakers" in the school, they then put into practice. The first step is to teach all students to negotiate constructive solutions to their conflicts. They learn "to define their conflict, exchange positions and proposals, view the situation from both perspectives, invent options for mutual gain, and reach a wise agreement." (p. 11) They practice the negotiation procedure through role-playing, becoming skillful in relatively easy situations. The next step is to teach all students the purposes and techniques of mediation, so that they can help classmates negotiate a constructive, mutually acceptable resolution to their conflicts. Some of the guidelines they learn are:

- Mediation is voluntary.

- Mediation does not occur unless both parties agree that they want to solve the problem.

- Each person has a chance to state his/her view of the conflict without interruption.

- Anything said in mediation is confidential.

If the conflicting parties agree to a solution, assisted by the student mediator, they are obliged to follow the agreement. Following the training, the teacher selects two class members to serve as mediators each day. They wear special tee shirts to identify them to their classmates. Students having conflicts they cannot solve take their problems to the mediator for assistance. Every student has a chance to serve as mediator; refresher lessons are taught once or twice a week to reinforce the negotiating and mediation skills.

What Did the Researchers Find?

During the period observed by the researchers, the frequency of student-student conflicts which were taken to the teacher for adjudication decreased by 80 percent. There were no conflicts taken to the principal for resolution. In their discussions with parents of the students involved in the Peacemaker Program, the researchers found that their students were using the techniques and approaches they had learned to handle conflicts with siblings at home and with children in the neighborhood. This substantiates one of the rationales of the program—that negotiating and mediating skills have many practical applications in life outside of the classroom and school. "Perhaps the most interesting evidence that the conflict training program worked was that many parents whose children were not part of the project requested that their children receive the training next year. A number of parents even requested training for themselves." (p. 13)

The researchers emphasize that the training must be thorough, so that students will begin to utilize the techniques and methods easily and naturally as they deal daily with on-the-spot conflicts. They insist that all students receive training and all students have the opportunity to serve as mediators, so it is not limited to those who might be perceived as teachers' pets or children with fewer conflicts or behavior problems.

What Are Possible Implications for School Improvement?

The Peacemaker Program shifts some of the responsibility for conflict resolution from the teacher and principal to the students. Traditionally, all conflicts are taken to the teacher or principal who then imposes a decision that might be arbitrary and unfair. S/he might not be able to take the time to hear all sides of the dispute in order to negotiate and mediate toward mutual agreement. The most expeditious procedure is to use the authority of the teacher or principal to force students to end the conflict. If that proves unsuccessful, teachers and administrators use a number of disciplinary procedures, from scolding and time-out rooms to more severe punishments, such as suspension or expulsion. Introducing a peer mediation program into a school can have a number of beneficial and positive outcomes. As students participate in the program and learn negotiation and mediation methods and skills, they develop self-discipline. They are strengthening their ability to assess a conflict situation and control their own behavior in the absence of external monitors. The training involved in this program encourages students to take responsibility for their own behavior, be aware of the needs of others, and be able to solve conflicts without always requiring the intervention of teacher or principal. "Students who know how to manage their conflicts constructively and regulate their own behavior have a developmental advantage over those who do not." (p. 11) This advantage will also carry over to their relationship and interactions in their families and neighborhoods.

The Peacemaker Program could be especially constructive in a school with a diverse student body representing many cultural, ethnic, social and language backgrounds. These students may be accustomed to using a variety of different procedures for managing conflict in the classroom and school. The training in negotiation and mediation, which this program requires, can teach students and staff to use the same set of procedures in managing conflicts. "Classrooms need to become places where destructive conflicts are prevented and where constructive conflicts are structured, encouraged, and utilized to improve the quality of instruction and classroom life." (p. 13) The empowerment of students to regulate and control their own and their classmates' actions will result in a decrease in the amount of time and energy which teachers and administrators must spend on student conflicts. And they, in turn, will be able to devote more effort to instruction and other educational matters.

— Nancy Berla

Note: For a description of a junior high school's experience with student mediation, see "Resolving Conflicts With Student Mediators" in Lawrence W. Lezotte and Barbara C. Jacoby (Eds.), *Effective Schools Practices That Work*. Effective Schools Products, Ltd., Okemos, MI, 1991, pp. 42–45.

EFFECTIVE SCHOOLS RESEARCH ABSTRACTS

SAFE AND ORDERLY ENVIRONMENT

CITATION: Stockard, Jean and Maralee Mayberry, *Effective Educational Environments*. Corwin Press, Inc., A Sage Publications Company, Newbury Park, CA, 1992.

What Did the Researchers Do?

The researchers reviewed and synthesized the contemporary literature that addresses the relationship between a student's learning environment and achievement. They considered learning environments important because, even after taking home and family influences into account and controlling for a school's socioeconomic level, schools still vary significantly in the quality of their services and in their students' level of achievement. The researchers focused on studies that examined the relationship between achievement and learning environment. They followed this approach, even though some research indicates that success in later life is more closely tied to how far one goes in school, rather than how much one actually learns in school.

The authors organized their analyses of environmental influences around four major areas: grouping of students, school and classroom learning climates, school facilities (especially school size), and community environments. Wherever possible, they emphasized studies that used large samples and better methodologies including several meta-analyses and detailed reviews.

What Did the Researchers Find?

Grouping of students. Virtually all instruction in school occurs in groups. The researchers found that the nature of the grouping does affect student achievement. Having more heterogeneous instructional groups produces the greatest achievement gains, especially for those who initially were not among the highest achievers. Generally, studies have found that desegregation enhances the achievement of minority students, especially when they begin desegregated schooling in kindergarten. "Students also show higher achievement in settings with more high-ability and high-status students and when they are not tracked into lower curricular areas

or low-ability groups." (p. 17) Although ability grouping may sometimes benefit high-achieving students, much of the research indicates that it impedes the progress of students in lower groups. Students placed in lower tracks (usually in high school) tend to develop lower self-esteem, lower aspirations, and more negative attitudes toward school. Tracking reproduces social class status by sorting students from different socioeconomic backgrounds into different curricula and then providing them with unequal learning environments. "The net effect of these various grouping practices is long term, as children in lower tracks and ability groups or in segregated schools fall progressively behind their same-age peers. The chances of catching up are slim." (p. 18)

School and classroom climate. The researchers found the following themes consistent throughout the review of the literature on school and classroom climate. Highly effective schools tend to emphasize teaching academic subjects, attaining subject matter competence, and acquiring basic skills. These schools value academic excellence; they expect their staffs to exhibit a high opinion of students' abilities.

Schools with teachers and students who see higher achievement as a real and attainable goal actually do have higher achievement. Effective school administrators promote both academic learning and cohesive relationships within a school; they have a high concern for both task accomplishments and cohesive social relations. Stable and consistent school environments appear strongest in schools where students and faculty participate in decision-making processes. This participation serves to enhance shared norms and values, which, in turn, helps create positive relationships among all school members. Students' achievements influence teachers' morale, sense of efficacy, and expectations for students. These, in turn, directly influence levels of student achievement. The researchers concluded that learning outcomes appear to be related to the ability of teachers and administrators to balance successfully the expressive (or socioemotional) and instrumental (or task-related) dimensions of both schools and classrooms.

Resources and school and classroom size. One of the most striking findings of the study was the lack of strong correlation between level of school expenditures and level of student achievement. Achievement appears to be related to the amount of time that students actually spend learning. Only one teacher characteristic, teacher's verbal ability, tends to show a consistent relationship with student achievement.

Smaller classrooms tend to be distinguished by their greater behavioral control, more individualized instruction, and more enriched curriculum. They may not cause higher achievement by themselves, but they do create conditions that make higher achievement possible, if and when teachers take full advantage of them. Smaller schools permit more opportunity for involvement, and they may make it easier for staff to reach consensus among both teachers and students, on curricular and disciplinary policies, compared to larger schools. Students in smaller schools tend to be characterized by their greater sense of personal efficacy, better self-concept, and heightened sense of self-control. While effective teaching is heavily dependent on the skills of the teacher, some environments are much more conducive to effective teaching than others. The conditions that enhance student achievement are also those that enhance effective teaching, higher teacher morale, and satisfaction.

Community environments and student achievement. "Schools in a community setting that promotes strong identification and ties between parents, students, and the school tend to be more likely to foster more effective school climates, once variables such as socioeconomic status of the parents are controlled." (p. 75) Good relationships between schools and parents and between the communities and their schools can enhance academic achievement, school climate, and school effectiveness. Conversely, when students are surrounded by people with low aspirations and achievement, their own aspirations tend to suffer. A large amount of evidence now supports the view that parental involvement is an important ingredient in improving individual children's achievement and in enhancing school effectiveness. Greater involvement of lower-income parents is more productive when teachers have more positive and understanding attitudes toward parents and develop the ability to communicate and work with parents in an open, collaborative manner.

The researchers conclude that students' achievement is enhanced when they attend school in a community with a large number of high-achieving peers, whose members interact with each other in a spirit of mutual respect and common values that support high achievement.

What Are Possible Implications for School Improvement?

Given the growing pressure for accountability for increased achievement, school leaders must look at all possible strategies for enhancing student learning. But they should also consider characteristics of the school environment that can enhance or impede increased learning. The willingness to alter the school learning environment itself has long been considered a characteristic of many effective schools. For example, even when a school has large classes and large pupil-teacher ratios, it can still use alternative scheduling and grouping structures in the school. Such strategies prove that it is possible to change the learning environment of students, to promote the school's mission of learning for all students. Systematically changing the climate in a school and its parent community cannot be done as a "quick fix." Such changes take time because they depend on a relationship of openness and trust which is often not present. When we set out to create a community of shared values, we know that no one has all the answers and everyone has a perspective that must be heard. These kinds of changes take time, but the dividends are great.

Probably the most significant conclusion to be drawn from this synthesis of the literature is that it reaffirms what the effective schools researchers have consistently maintained from the beginning: schools do control enough of the variables that affect student learning. Schools can increase that learning significantly, if the school staffs are motivated to do so and are willing to change some of their adult behaviors and organizational procedures.

— Lawrence W. Lezotte

EFFECTIVE SCHOOLS RESEARCH ABSTRACTS

SAFE AND ORDERLY ENVIRONMENT

CITATION: Cheng, Yin Cheong, "Profiles of School Culture and Effective Schools," *School Effectiveness and School Improvement* 4, 2 (May 1993): 85-110.

What Did the Researcher Do?

The culture of schools, the culture of organizations, is a topic of great interest to many. The effective schools correlate, Safe and Orderly Environment, deals with a school's culture—both in the narrow sense of student behavior and in the broad sense of adult behavior. Yet, there are very few studies that specifically relate a school's culture to the academic achievement of its students.

Is a school's organizational culture related to different aspects of leadership behavior, job attitudes of teachers, and students' academic outcomes?

To answer this question, the researcher surveyed 588 randomly selected teachers in 54 secondary schools in Hong Kong. They responded to instruments which measured organizational characteristics (i.e., organizational culture, organizational structure, and leadership style), job attitudes of teachers, and school effectiveness. The psychometric properties of the instruments, including reliability and validity, were established in prior studies and in the current study. In addition to the instruments, student performance on standardized tests in the Chinese language, the English language, and mathematics was examined. The unit of analysis was the school.

What Did the Researcher Find?

The organizational culture of a school is strongly correlated with effectiveness as perceived by teachers. Principals' charisma and teachers' esprit are significant factors when predicting a school's organizational ideology. The more principals can provide teachers with meaning and inspiration for their work, the stronger the organizational culture. The more teachers are enthusiastic about their work, the stronger the sharing of beliefs in the school.

The researcher identified 16 strong culture and 16 weak culture schools among the 54 schools studied. The strong culture schools had statistically significantly higher mean scores on nine of the 11 organizational culture variables. These schools had statistically significantly higher mean scores on eight of the eight job attitudes of teachers variables. Organizational effectiveness, as perceived by teachers, was significantly higher in the strong culture schools. Student academic achievement was higher, but not significantly so, in the strong culture schools.

The researcher then identified 16 effective and 16 ineffective schools. The pattern of differences between them was very similar to the pattern of differences between the strong and weak culture schools.

Next, the researcher identified 11 strong culture-effective schools, 13 weak culture-ineffective schools, and one weak culture-effective school. (He did not find any strong culture-ineffective schools.) He found that overall student academic achievement was statistically significantly higher in the strong culture-effective schools than it was in the weak culture-ineffective schools.

These two types of schools are substantially different. The strong culture-effective schools have much higher levels of clear and consistent beliefs about the schools' mission, goal, and role. There is a more formalized organizational culture that encourages teacher participation in decision-making and staff development activities.

Principals in strong culture-effective schools tend to initiate structure (i.e., "the extent to which patterns of organization, communication, and working procedures are established"). (p. 102) These principals are also more willing to foster friendship and respect between themselves and teachers. These principals have charisma; they are able to inspire their staffs and give meaning to the work of their teachers.

Teachers in strong culture-effective schools have higher morale, higher commitment to the school, and higher satisfaction with intrinsic rewards. These teachers welcome the opportunities for personal growth that their jobs offer and enjoy more friendly social relations with their colleagues.

The researcher found it "interesting to explore the characteristics of…[the one school perceived as the weak culture-effective school]. It is different from the strong culture-effective schools or the weak culture-ineffective schools…This school is characterized mainly by the serious lack of organizational culture and the principal's great emphasis on task with little consideration to the teachers." (p. 100) Under the "unbalanced production-oriented leadership and strong structure, this school may be perceived by its teachers as productive and may also have good academic achievements in the public examination. But in terms of job attitudes, the performance of teachers seems to be poor in most aspects…we may worry whether this school can remain effective in the long run." (p. 100)

What Are Possible Implications for School Improvement?

Schools make a difference! The 54 schools studied were "relatively homogeneous in terms of salary structure, professional qualification of teachers and administrators…teacher-class ratios, school facilities, formal curricula…public examination…formal opportunities of professional training and development, and supervision by the Hong Kong Education Department. (pp. 88–89) However, some schools had significantly higher student academic achievement than others. Also, the group of schools with better student performance was substantially different than the schools with lower student performance.

More important, when these differences between the two types of schools are examined, they collapse back into the correlates of Instructional Leadership, Clear and Focused School Mission, and Safe and Orderly Environment (when this correlate is defined in terms of the teachers' culture). This is consistent with Lezotte's description of the Second Generation of this correlate. He wrote: "It is unlikely that a school's faculty could successfully teach its students to work together unless the adults in the school model collaborative behaviors in their own professional working relationships."[1]

Moreover, to increase student learning, educators must pay attention to improving the culture of the school. The strong culture-effective schools have a substantially different culture than the weak culture-ineffective schools. It is significant that the researcher concluded that the one weak culture-effective school studied probably will not continue to be effective because of poor teacher attitudes and social relationships.

It is commonly assumed in this country that the way to improve student achievement is to concentrate heavily on the subject area or areas of concern (e.g., defined student outcomes, curriculum alignment, an aligned authentic assessment program, changed teaching behaviors) to the exclusion of almost everything else. An example can be seen in the major effort that is under way in one state to improve student achievement in all subject areas. It puts special emphasis on reading, writing, science, and mathematics. In this state, the department of education is strongly encouraging schools to develop school improvement plans centered almost entirely upon the specific academic areas of concern. The state's model for school improvement plans places almost no emphasis on changing the culture of the school to incorporate what is known about the relationship between school cultures and sustained high levels of student achievement. The state's model format for school improvement plans strongly emphasizes issues such as defined student outcomes, curriculum alignment, etc. These important issues are necessary, but not sufficient. The need to support and sustain high levels of achievement is being ignored not only in this state, but in other states as well. The effective schools research (of which Cheng's study is a part) shows that to improve and maintain student achievement, attention must be paid to key variables in the culture of a school—better known as the correlates.

— Robert E. Sudlow

---

[1] Lezotte, Lawrence W., "Correlates of Effective Schools: The First and Second Generations"; also Lezotte, Lawrence, and Barbara C. Jacoby, *Sustainable School Reform: The District Context for School Improvement.* Effective Schools Products, Ltd., Okemos, MI, 1992.

EFFECTIVE SCHOOLS RESEARCH ABSTRACTS

SAFE AND ORDERLY ENVIRONMENT

CITATION: Gottfredson, Denise C., Gary D. Gottfredson, and Lois G. Hybl, "Managing Adolescent Behavior: A Multiyear Multischool Study," *American Educational Research Journal* 30, 1 (Spring 1993): 179-215.

What Did the Researchers Do?

In this article, the authors "review what is known about the nature and causes of student misbehavior, describe a middle-school program designed to reduce misbehavior, and report the results of a three-year study to assess the program's effect in six middle schools." (p. 180) The program was developed to "attempt to cope with a crisis of student misconduct that was produced by the accumulation in the middle schools of large numbers of students with diminished investment in education." (p. 182) In this particular study, conducted in the Charleston (South Carolina) County School District, the numbers of these students had increased, due to a "get tough" approach to education. This included raising standards for grade promotion, which increased grade retention. The resulting increase in middle school students who were at least one year behind grade level apparently raised the levels of student disattachment and misconduct.

What Did the Researchers Find?

Adolescent misconduct usually is not specialized; that is, students who have behavior difficulties in school also exhibit problems in the community and at home. In school, a common response to misconduct has been the use of out-of-school suspension. Suspension limits the opportunities students have to learn, and teachers may lower their expectations for troublesome students. Peers of these students may avoid the misbehaving students, leaving them only the more deviant peer groups for socialization.

"Misbehavior in school has both individual and environmental determinants. Some environmental characteristics raise the probability of disorderly behavior in the environment and some personal characteristics make it more likely that a particular individual will misbehave." (p. 181)

Classroom. Important factors in maintaining classroom order are teachers' clarity of communication; styles of monitoring and responding to student behavior; extent of student responsibility and accountability for work; and methods of organizing instruction. "Some teachers are more likely to produce higher levels of misconduct in their classroom by their management and organization practices." (p. 182)

School. Some schools tend to be more orderly in nature, which leads to better overall student conduct. Orderly schools have a "clear focus on appropriate student behavior; clear expectations for behavior; much communication about the rules, sanctions, and procedures to be used; formal discipline codes and classroom management plans; and expressed concern for students as individuals." (p. 182)

Individual student. Misbehaving students are more likely to be male than female; display less academic competence; dislike school; have more delinquent friends; have limited career and educational objectives; believe less in conventional social rules; and display poor interpersonal relations. They are less likely to defer to adult authority and are deficient in problem-solving skills.

In an attempt to improve student behavior, the Charleston County program incorporated interventions at the school, classroom, and individual level, all of which were aimed at reducing the misbehavior of middle school students.

School interventions. School improvement teams revised their school discipline policies to increase rule clarity and specified the consequences for specific infractions in order to achieve consistency in schoolwide and individual classroom policies. The teams then oriented their faculties to the program and developed strategies for schoolwide implementation. A computerized tracking system was devised to record every positive and negative referral to the office. This information was used to generate reports for administrators and facilitated more frequent communication with parents about both positive and negative student school behaviors.

Classroom interventions. School improvement team members attended a workshop "to learn about the classroom organization and management and behavior change strategies. They then organized and carried out staff development workshops covering these strategies for teachers in their schools, monitored implementation of the new strategies in their colleagues' classrooms, and provided constructive feedback and ongoing technical support of their colleagues as they implemented the new practices." (p. 185)

Individual-level interventions. This component of the program "was based on the assumption that misbehavior results in part because the environment reinforces undesirable behaviors and fails to reinforce desirable behaviors." (p. 184) Each team created a student handbook describing school rules and consequences for violations. In some schools, they also incorporated a system of rewards for appropriate behavior (for example, a student-of-the-month contest). Schools also used the computerized management system to generate letters to inform parents of positive teacher referrals. The positive reinforcement aspect was individualized creatively by the school team. Other examples included assigning high-risk youths to volunteer teachers who monitored the students' behavior by having each student carry a "report card" from class to class, where each teacher would rate the student on the target behavior. A designated teacher saw each of these students daily and provided some type of reinforcement at the end of each successful day. A more substantial reward was provided at the end of each successful week with a pizza party. In some schools, bulletin boards featured successful students.

The program involved an integrated approach to discipline management that provided a mix of activities targeting the entire school, classrooms within the school, and individuals within the school. It was anticipated that these integrated interventions would produce a larger effect on student behavior than targeting only individual factors, such as individual students or classrooms.

What Are Possible Implications for School Improvement?

There were variances in implementation which had an impact on the program's reported effectiveness.

For example, five of the six schools experienced at least one change in administrators during the project period. Administrative support for the program varied from weak support to strong support and leadership. When the results were analyzed, those schools that enjoyed administrative support with no visible signs of implementation breakdown experienced the most improvement in several of the outcome measures of the study. When the program was well implemented, school discipline policy review and revision, computerized behavior tracking, improved organization and management, and positive reinforcement of good behavior "were blended together by the school team to create an integrated discipline management system for the school. The program took on a different character in each school as the teams molded it to fit their local environments." (p. 185)

This study implies that schools can intervene to improve student behavior. However, this approach to improving student conduct in the middle grades may be limited by the differing capacity of schools to implement such large-scale changes. The level of administrative support for the program and the team appears to be related to the degree of success of implementation.

In order to produce a coherent change in student behavior, it is necessary to examine the underlying approach to student discipline. Simply clarifying school discipline policies, implementing a computerized behavior management system, and developing a school-level system for rewarding appropriate behavior is not enough. While these activities may produce an increase in students' reports of clarity of rules and rewards, they will not reduce student misconduct and rebellious behavior. Some schools in the study undertook these activities, but also significantly reduced the amount of punishment and changed the school climate. Schools that fostered "respectful, supportive, and fair treatment of students experienced beneficial student outcomes." (p. 209)

If schools truly want to reduce student misbehavior, they would be well advised to consider the findings of this study. Success in reducing student misbehavior requires administrative and staff commitment during the study process, followed by assistance and support during implementation.

— Lee Gerard

EFFECTIVE SCHOOLS RESEARCH ABSTRACTS

SAFE AND ORDERLY ENVIRONMENT

CITATION: Wang, Margaret C., Geneva D. Haertel, and Herbert J. Walberg, "What Helps Students Learn?" *Educational Leadership* 51, 4 (December 1993-January 1994): 74-79.

What Did the Researchers Do?

What makes a difference in accounting for student learning? Is it a direct influence, such as the amount of time a teacher spends on a topic? Or is it an indirect influence, such as a school or district policy, or even something as indirect as site-based management, the current buzzword in the educational reform movement? To answer these questions, the researchers analyzed the content of 179 handbook chapters and reviews, synthesized 91 research summaries, and contacted 61 educational researchers. From these three broad sources, they built a knowledge base of 11,000 statistical findings that indicated the most important effects on learning. Though the studies varied in sample size, rigor, and characteristics, the authors used a meta-analysis to analyze and express the data in the form of averages or mean effects.

To summarize their findings, the researchers developed a 28-category conceptual framework. The 28 categories included such psychological factors as student ability and motivation, classroom variables such as enthusiasm, clarity, and feedback, as well as out-of-school attributes such as social-psychological influences. The categories were then rank ordered. To clarify the most significant influences, the researchers grouped the 28 categories into broad types of influences: student aptitude, classroom instruction and climate, context, program design, school organization, and state and district characteristics. These broad groups were also rank ordered.

What Did the Researchers Find?

What do 50 years of research tell us about the impact of the various components on student learning? "In general, we found that direct influences have a greater impact on learning than indirect influences. Direct influences include the amount of time a teacher spends on a topic and the quality of the social interactions teachers have with their students. Indirect influences include policies adopted by a school district, or state, and organizational features such as site-based management." (p. 74)

Among the six broad groupings of types of influence, student aptitude is the most effective. Of the six categories within this top group, "a student's metacognitive processes—that is, a student's capacity to plan, monitor, and, if necessary, re-plan learning strategies—had the most powerful effect on his or her learning." (p. 75) Research in metacognitive processes has sparked such innovations as reciprocal teaching and cognitive instruction. The second most influential category in the student aptitude group is cognitive processes. It includes such variables as general intelligence, prior knowledge, competency in reading and math, and verbal knowledge. The third most influential category in this group was social and behavioral characteristics, such as positive, nondisruptive behavior, which contribute to performing well. (This surely makes sense!) In a similar ranking, motivational and affective attributes, such as effort and perseverance, long recognized by teachers as key determinants of learning, are also recognized here by researchers as necessary for self-controlled, self-regulated learners. Categories of least importance in this top group are psychomotor skills and student demographics, such as gender and socioeconomic status.

Classroom instruction and climate had almost as much influence on student learning as student aptitude. Of the eight categories in this second group, the most influential is classroom management, with a mean of 64.8—the highest of all 28 categories. Such effective classroom management techniques as "group alerting, learner accountability, smooth transitions, and teacher 'with-it-ness' increases student engagement, decreases disruptive behaviors, and makes good use of instructional time." (p. 76)

Next in effectiveness in this group is constructive student and teacher social interactions. It is characterized by positive student responses to questions and comments from the teacher and other students. The extensive research also documents that quantity of instruction, classroom climate, and classroom instruction have a significant impact on student learning. Of more moderate effect are academic interactions, consisting of teachers' styles for questions, praise and reinforcement, and classroom assessment. Though many studies indicated that frequent assessment and feedback effectively promoted learning, "some researchers…were concerned about national and state assessments and outcome-based education driving educational reform. The mixture of these good results and grave concerns probably accounted for the moderate rating for assessment." (p. 76) Of least importance in this classroom instruction group is classroom implementation and support. It consists of delivery of instructional services, staff development, and the adequate training of teachers. This is one of the categories "perceived by educators as important, but…[its] weak influence on student learning…may reflect the lack of implementation of its variables rather than its relative influence. Although teachers may receive training on how to implement a particular practice or innovation, they may not be successful at putting these practices into action." (pp. 76–77)

The context group consists of four out-of-school categories. It is almost as influential on student learning as student aptitude and classroom instruction and climate. The home environment/parental support category in this group is fourth highest of all 28 categories. "The benefits of family involvement in improving students' academic performance have been well documented, as have its effects on improving school attendance and on reducing delinquency, pregnancies, and dropping out." (p. 77) The current research also documents the importance of the peer group category that includes the academic aspirations of peers. The community influences category is less influential, perhaps because of limited empirical research. The least important category in this group is out-of-class time (consisting of student extracurricular activities and social clubs).

It is interesting that the program design group, consisting of well-designed textbooks, appropriate organization of instructional groups, and effective alignment of goals and classroom activities had only a moderate influence on learning.

The school organization group emphasizes various governance and administrative matters. The most influential of its five categories is school culture, "an ethos conducive to teaching and learning," that emphasizes a schoolwide focus on academic achievement. (p. 78)

The last group, state and district characteristics, consists of state-level policies, such as guidelines for the development and selection of curricula and textbooks, and district demographics. The latter, which includes "per-pupil expenditure, contractual limits on class size, and the degree of school district bureaucracy," is the least influential of the 28 categories that were studied. (p. 78)

What Are Possible Implications for School Improvement?

This comprehensive summary of 50 years of research on student learning is clearly organized and succinctly presented. Of its many valuable insights, let's consider two. First, the evidence from this study clearly indicates that those variables such as the categories in the student aptitude and classroom instruction and climate groups that have a direct impact on student learning are the most effective. Thus, when time and money are available, these resources should be channeled into projects to improve, for example, both the teaching of students' metacognitive processes and classroom management. Second, the data presented in this study also forcibly indicate that variables that are the most removed from classroom application (such as school restructuring and organizational factors) have the least effect on student learning. Many of the current reform movements, such as school-based management, may not merit the time and effort required to implement them, say the researchers. By carefully considering the research, districts can become better informed in getting their priorities in order to allocate their time, efforts, and monies where they will do the most good for their children. Educators taking this challenge seriously will find much to ponder in this article's concise definitions and useful rank ordering of the 28 categories of influence on student learning.

— Frank X. Ferris

EFFECTIVE SCHOOLS RESEARCH ABSTRACTS

SAFE AND ORDERLY ENVIRONMENT

CITATION: Brantlinger, Ellen, "Social Class in School: Students' Perspectives," *Research Bulletin 14*, Phi Delta Kappa, Center for Evaluation, Development, and Research, March 1995.

What Did the Researcher Do?

How do students from diverse economic and social backgrounds perceive their role and status in the school? In what ways does background affect the attitudes of students toward teachers, peers, and themselves, as well as the likelihood that they will experience educational success? How do school personnel, policies, and practices influence the feelings and attitudes of students from high-income and low-income families?

This research examined how students react to disparities and inequalities in the school and how their economic and social background affects their perceptions and attitudes. The study is based on three interrelated ideas and assumptions: (1) it is important to understand the attitudes affecting student behavior; (2) social class influences students' attitudes about education; and (3) views of social class affect the dynamics of schools and classrooms.

The subjects were high school students, age 13 to 18, in a mid-size Midwestern town. Thirty-four students from middle-class suburbs were selected for the high-income sample, and 40 students whose families live in government-subsidized housing comprised the low-income sample. Both groups were similar in terms of race, age, and grade level. Participants were interviewed using open-ended questions to elicit responses about social class and schooling.

Prior to enrollment in high school, the two groups were "segregated in virtually all aspects of daily life." (p. 1) They lived in separate neighborhoods and attended different elementary schools. In the low-income housing areas, those schools were in old, run-down buildings with small, poorly equipped playgrounds. The principals and teachers had inferior training and experience. Both part-time staff and high student-teacher ratios were more common than in the middle-class elementary schools.

What Did the Researcher Find?

The status of the elementary schools was well known at the secondary level and affected how students were labeled when they entered high school. Homogeneous grouping or tracking and the assignment of students from low-income families to special education continued the separation between the two groups. "The result of little contact was that students held stereotyped and unrealistic views of each other—views that prevented subsequent interaction." (p. 1) Interview responses revealed that both groups identified each other similarly: "haves and have nots, rich and poor, grits and preps, smart and dumb, and good and bad kids." (p. 2)

In the low-income group, 28 out of 40 currently or previously were in special education classes; only three were placed in advanced tracks. In the high-income group, all students, even those with learning disabilities, were assigned to the college preparatory curriculum. According to the interviews, low-income students considered placement in special education as humiliating, resulting in peer rejection and lack of popularity. One remarked that "being in special education tells other people that you're dumb." (p. 2) High-income students favored ability grouping and tracking and believed that they deserved to be assigned to the higher groups.

The attitudes of the two groups toward their teachers provides further evidence of social class disparities. High-income students took positive relations with teachers for granted, although many of them expressed their superiority over their teachers and showed cynicism and indifference toward them. The low-income students generally perceived most teachers as affluent, did not like them, and believed they preferred the "preppies." These students were especially appreciative of the few teachers who were kind to them.

The middle-class students had negative attitudes toward the low-income group, which itself held similar perceptions about the shortcomings and deficits of peers. The responses from both groups reflected the similar belief that individual characteristics play a predominant role in determining economic well-being.

The view that personal characteristics within a person's control are responsible for poverty was held by 57.5 percent of the low-income students and 70 percent of the high-income students. Thirty percent of both groups believed that the conditions causing poverty are beyond an individual's control. In both groups, 60 percent stated the belief that people are wealthy because of factors within their control, while 40 percent felt that achieving affluence is beyond an individual's control.

High-income students viewed lower-class students as prone to violence. In an analysis of conflicts between the two groups, the researcher found that the middle-class students were often the aggressors, provoking retaliation from lower-class students, who usually were the ones caught and punished.

The school experience was a major source of stress for low-income students, whose dreams for achievement and a better life were quickly dampened by school policies and practices. They were assigned to the low tracks or special education classes, experienced failing grades, and felt peer and teacher rejection regularly. They often concluded that their inadequacies or unworthiness were the reasons for their mistreatment.

What Are Possible Implications for School Improvement?

According to Ron Edmonds, "we can, whenever and wherever we choose, successfully teach all children whose schooling is of interest to us. We already know more than we need to do that. Whether or not we do it must finally depend on how we feel about the fact that we haven't so far."

This research can be useful to school administrators and teachers who want to understand why students are angry and alienated toward education. The beliefs, feelings, and perspectives of low-income students are well documented here and offer insights into the negative aspects of the school environment they encounter. School personnel should become aware of and sensitive to policies and practices based on assumptions about the weaknesses and inferiority of students from low-income families. Furthermore, understanding the feelings of lower-class students as they experience inequities in school might change the views of those who see special education classes and ability grouping as beneficial to students with weaker educational backgrounds.

The researcher suggests a few strategies for improving school climate: promote integration, encourage student participation in school governance, and create schools within schools. These are laudable objectives, but may be too general and abstract to affect the daily experience of most students. Major changes in special education placement and tracking policies should be considered, along with such programs as peer mediation of student conflicts.

The public schools may portray themselves as democratic, classless institutions, but the researcher points out that "school is not a socially neutral setting." (p. 3) Middle- and upper-class students receive privileged treatment from school personnel, who themselves are members of the middle class. Students from low-income families have second-class status at school and begin to accept and internalize the belief in their own inferiority and personal inadequacy. Their lack of confidence and low self-esteem inevitably play a major role in deciding whether to stay in school or drop out.

— Nancy Berla

EFFECTIVE SCHOOLS RESEARCH ABSTRACTS

SAFE AND ORDERLY ENVIRONMENT

CITATION: Wade, Rahima C., "Encouraging Student Initiative in a Fourth-Grade Classroom," *Elementary School Journal* 95 (March 1995): 339-354.

What Did the Researcher Do?

How can the classroom teacher create opportunities for more student-centered, empowered learning experiences? Will students respond favorably or resist greater involvement in their own education? Will empowerment help students become adults who challenge the status quo, seek solutions to problems, and speak their minds in public forums?

The traditional classroom operates as a hierarchy, with the teacher responsible for making all decisions about curriculum topics and what students should learn. This study was an effort to restructure curriculum planning in order to give students opportunities to initiate classroom learning. Such empowerment could be expected to enhance students' ability to act effectively and responsibly in their life outside school.

Through active participation in a 4th grade classroom in a suburban public school in New Hampshire, the researcher chronicled the curricular events that fostered or inhibited empowerment of the 17 students and explored the factors influencing empowerment efforts.

A review of the literature revealed a number of definitions of student empowerment by "social activists, critical theorists, feminist scholars, educational reformers, and community organizers." (p. 340) Many scholars have written about the concept in a theoretical or abstract way, but few have studied it at the classroom level in a traditional public school. The definition used in this study is that empowerment involves "the development of confidence and efficacy, as well as skills in self-expression, organization, decision-making, and communication." (p. 342) It encompasses both individual and group goals, as well as social and personal expectations.

The researcher was a classroom participant from October 1990 until June 1991. The teacher had 10 years of experience, was a friend of the researcher, and had "strong concerns for students' rights and responsibilities and wanted her students to initiate their own learning in her classroom." (p. 342) The data were gathered through observations in the school and classroom, discussions and interviews with teachers and students, audiotapes of classroom events, and logs kept by the researcher.

What Did the Researcher Find?

Although the classroom operated in a conventional or traditional manner, the researcher identified two main themes in teaching style that supported and encouraged student empowerment. The teacher (1) respected the personal experiences and ideas of pupils as individuals and (2) emphasized positive social relations, trying to mediate and use inductive reasoning to handle any misbehavior or disciplinary problems. The teaching style was more student centered than in many of the classrooms at the school; students had much freedom in deciding the order of their assignments and whether to work alone or with a friend on class projects. Collaboration on assignments was encouraged, but the teacher considered knowledge acquisition as primarily an individual pursuit.

The "experiment" began in January, when the teacher and researcher established a democratic system. A class meeting was scheduled each week, and three students helped the researcher plan and facilitate the meeting. An agenda for discussion or action was proposed by the teacher, the researcher, and the students. At the weekly meetings between January and June, nine students proposed 19 of the 28 agenda items, many of which related to fairness and equal treatment (stolen pencils, accusations of wrongdoing, and playground behavior are examples).

One of the most successful projects was the creation of a class Bill of Rights. The students brainstormed possible rights in small groups and then voted on them as a group. The list included rights to personal safety, protection of property, a quiet work space, respect from teachers, and free time after schoolwork was completed. As part of this project, the students petitioned the principal for the rights to wear hats and to chew gum in the classroom. He responded a week later, denying permission to chew gum because that was a privilege reserved for fifth graders, but approving the wearing of hats.

Another set of activities to enhance student empowerment was service projects. The researcher suggested and implemented the first one, making puppets to send to India to teach villagers how to cure diarrhea in young children. Only one service project was initiated by students—a brownie sale to benefit a local soup kitchen. Other proposals did not elicit sufficient student or adult support and were not pursued.

Three factors were identified as limiting the development of student initiatives. First, the school climate emphasized discipline, order, and teacher-centered instruction. Second, students received many mixed messages from the teacher, researcher, and principal. The researcher and teacher held different beliefs, perceptions, and values. The teacher was reluctant to give full support to student freedom since this was her first year at that grade level. Student suggestions for new projects often were not given enough support from the adults in the classroom. Third, students were accustomed to the principal and teacher being the primary decision makers and did not shift into the role of initiators easily or comfortably. The researcher did observe, however, that self-confidence and leadership ability clearly increased in some students.

According to the researcher, three elements are critical to student empowerment in the classroom:

- Teachers must fully support student participation in decision making.

- Teachers must demonstrate their support by explicit actions to foster empowerment.

- A feeling of ownership by students of learning and/or service projects is critical to their interest and participation.

What Are Possible Implications for School Improvement?

This article provides teachers and administrators with several promising ideas. The institutional and personnel factors that encourage or inhibit student empowerment are identified. Educators who endorse greater student participation in curriculum planning and implementation will find these results useful.

The study suggests that it may be difficult for teachers and administrators to change from the traditional approach. In order to take the risks associated with a shift in power to the students, teachers must have confidence in the value of student empowerment, as well as support from the school administration.

It would be interesting to have additional research on whether student empowerment affects performance, attendance, and attitudes toward education. Those who study and write about dropouts often mention alienation as a factor in the decision to leave school. Would student empowerment in upper elementary grades, middle schools, and high schools help develop a feeling of ownership toward the curriculum, assignments, and projects? Experiences such as those described in this article may enable students to understand the importance of education and increase their willingness to stay in school.

— Nancy Berla

EFFECTIVE SCHOOLS RESEARCH ABSTRACTS

SAFE AND ORDERLY ENVIRONMENT

CITATION: Cohn, Carl A., "Mandatory School Uniforms," *The School Administrator* 2 (February 1996): 22-25.

What Did the Researcher Do?

Two years ago, the Long Beach Unified School District in Long Beach, California became the first school system in the nation to require uniforms in all elementary and middle schools. Though "much of the public school educational establishment reacted skeptically" at first, a substantial decrease in school crime turned these skeptics into supporters of the uniform policy. (p. 22)

The defeat in the Fall of 1993 of Proposition 174, a statewide school voucher initiative which would have provided public funds for private schools, had a strong impact on the decision to make school uniforms a requirement. Although the proposal was defeated, citizens expressed deep concern about the effectiveness of public schools. The Long Beach Unified School District School Board members participated in some of those debates and promised the community that, if Proposition 174 was defeated, significant improvements would be made in the district.

Those who supported the voucher system had many criticisms of the public schools, including the comment that "even when some individual schools get better, the leadership doesn't have the courage to bring the reforms to the whole system." (pp. 22-23) Board members in Long Beach recognized the legitimacy of this concern because there was already a highly successful school uniform program at 11 of the 70 elementary and middle schools that were piloting the initiative. Soon after the defeat of Proposition 174, the school board unanimously agreed to require uniforms in all elementary and middle schools, with a starting date of September 1994.

What Did the Researcher Find?

As a result of the district's commitment to make student safety a priority, and to have mandatory school uniforms at the elementary and middle school levels as a key part of the emphasis on a safe and orderly learning environment, several changes have been observed. "Gang clothing is virtually nonexistent. Our uniforms thus provide a safe passage for children who must negotiate their way through gang territories going to and from school." (p. 23) Students and parents do not need to worry about choosing colors or styles of clothing that might inadvertently indicate the child is a gang member. The uniforms also allow school personnel to easily identify outsiders who do not belong on school grounds. The potential for violence is greater when youth from outside the school have ready access to the school grounds.

At the end of the first year of the program, the district's data showed a significant drop in the incidences of fighting, assaults, robberies, vandalism, and weapons possession. Overall, there was a 36 percent decrease in crime districtwide at the K-8 level after one year of the program. Suspensions also dropped in the first year of the program.

All parts of the district, both urban and suburban, have benefited from mandatory school uniforms. Minority and majority parents support the program as a way to "help foster a professional mindset for students. Children in uniform come to school with the attitude they are coming to school to work. School is then seen as a workplace for teaching and learning." (p. 24)

The district has found that the "average clothing cost per child in schools with a student uniform is markedly less than that in schools without a uniform program, reducing clothing costs for parents." (p. 24) Typical cost in the district for three uniforms is $70-90 per year.

For those interested in adopting a mandatory school uniform policy, the author cites five critical conditions that he deems necessary in the community before going forward. They are:

- **A stable school board.** Major policy changes which directly affect all students must be made in a stable board environment where a consensus can be achieved and maintained.

- **Supportive parents and community.** Early in the process, the Long Beach Press-Telegram conducted a survey which found 80 percent of parents and community members in favor of the idea of school uniforms. This was "contrary to the conventional wisdom that urban school parents do not support higher dress standards." (p. 25)

- **Resources to defend the policy.** The district must not undertake an important, but controversial, approach without allocating resources to defend it from legal challenges.

- **Capable site administrators.** Principals must provide enthusiastic support for the initiative or there will not be a high rate of compliance.

- **Community philanthropic resources.** These resources and service organizations help make sure that poor students have basic school necessities, including school uniforms. (p. 25)

What Are Possible Implications for School Improvement?

If school improvement is to occur, the school environment must support it. While it may be possible for some children to learn well in an unsafe and chaotic environment (some students succeed despite their school environment), it is clear that student achievement levels and a teacher's ability to teach are adversely affected by unsafe or disorderly schools.

When selecting improvement strategies which impact the school climate, it is important to monitor how well the strategies are helping the school to accomplish its purpose. In the case of the Long Beach district, data after the program's first year clearly showed improvement in the safety and orderliness of the school, which can, in turn, impact learning.

It is also important to be mindful of the prerequisites to instituting major policy changes, especially those which are controversial, so that success is more likely to occur. Understanding community attitudes and soliciting parent and community support at the beginning of the process are vital first steps.

— Lynn Benore

EFFECTIVE SCHOOLS RESEARCH ABSTRACTS

SAFE AND ORDERLY ENVIRONMENT

CITATION: Heller, Gary S., "Changing the School to Reduce Student Violence: What Works?" *NASSP Bulletin* 80 (April 1996): 1-10.

What Did the Researcher Do?

"One need only read the daily newspaper or tune into the evening news broadcast to be informed of acts of violence in our schools." (p. 1) According to the author, a principal at a senior high school, there are two types of schools: "those that have had a significant incident and those that will." (p. 1) Even so, he points out that a well-formulated plan can significantly "reduce acts of student violence, in both number and intensity." (p. 2)

The author stresses that "the entire school organization must be designed to support and encourage student responsibility and to address those issues and behaviors that are not conducive to instructional and academic success." (p. 2) He reports on the measures taken in his high school in Central Valley, New York to establish an effective program which focuses on school assessment, student management, intervention strategies, and alternative education.

What Did the Researcher Find?

Well-disciplined schools do not happen by accident. They start by using research findings which have been proven successful in other schools.

For example, well-disciplined schools identify clear, concise, and relevant curriculum goals. Curriculum is viewed as a "living document" and is periodically evaluated and modified. (p. 2) Staff members see themselves as student advocates. All student management programs emphasize positive student behaviors, student responsibility, and preventive measures.

Research and practice have shown the necessity for staff, students, and community to work together. A well-disciplined school expends time and energy in order to create and maintain this cooperative spirit.

Well-disciplined schools also put extraordinary emphasis on organizational variables. The most prominent variable includes the attitudes, interests, and commitment of staff members. Full staff involvement, with the principal as facilitator of teacher-initiated discipline and intervention strategies, is indicative of the movement away from the traditional practices of stern, rigid administrative intervention of rules enforcement.

Well-disciplined schools realize that it is often difficult, if not impossible, to do the job alone. Therefore, other resources, such as police departments, courts, welfare organizations, etc., are purposefully involved as needed.

Assessment of school needs. The safety and security of the school should be regularly assessed by students, staff, and the community. This assessment provides essential data as to the real or perceived needs of the school or district.

Student management issues must be analyzed through the use of objective data, collected over a period of time. Incident reports covering truancy, substance abuse, fighting, vandalism, and other topics can be used to point out recurring problem areas. "School personnel should not fear the results of these surveys. They are the key to addressing the needs of the school and should be shared with constituent groups that possess the power to provide needed resources." (p. 4)

Student management. Well-disciplined schools are sensitive to their students' racial and socioeconomic concerns. All students are informed and are aware of their rights and responsibilities. Students are reminded of the school's rules and regulations and associated behavioral consequences—both at the start of and throughout the school year. Also, staff members are skilled at identifying at-risk students and possess a wide range of intervention strategies. These schools value research which shows that school climate and available school activities have a profound positive effect on school discipline.

Consistency of the application of a rule is usually good advice. However, "sometimes, the key to a successful intervention with a particular student is his or her understanding and realization that someone, finally, really listened and took his or her concerns and problems into consideration." (p. 5)

Intervention strategies. The author mentions numerous intervention strategies which have been successfully initiated at his school:

- Anger Management Seminar teaches socially appropriate skills to help students (and parents) deal with anger.

- Human Understanding and Growth (H.U.G.) Program provides information on various aspects of adolescent development (drug abuse, peer pressure, etc.).

- Partners Acting as Instructional Resources (P.A.I.R.) Program pairs volunteer faculty members with selected students in a "big brother/big sister" format.

- Pupil Personnel Services evaluates selected students through a child study team, with recommendations made for intervention.

- Student Awareness Sessions bring peer mediators and student council members together to meet with all classes to discuss acceptable problem-solving alternatives.

- A review of the disciplinary code, using data on student suspensions, is conducted yearly by students, staff, parents, and community members.

- Staff development, including information and strategies on student management, is made available to all staff members.

- Supervision is provided by all staff members who are expected to monitor hallways, lunch areas, study halls, etc.

Alternative education. Since some students will not be able to find success in a traditional four-year high school, opportunities must be made available so all students can learn. Suggestions include individual placement classes, use of the resources of a county center, or use of the school building after the regular school day.

What Are Possible Implications for School Improvement?

None of the intervention strategies mentioned in this article are unique. However, several statements clearly indicate the realistic thinking of the school administrators which, undoubtedly, contribute to the success of the programs. "Before school administrators can address the issues of school violence, they must realize that in some cases they will be dealing with student and family problems that are beyond their ability to control or manage. Schools will never be able to totally eliminate all acts of student violence; any other belief is unrealistic." (p. 2)

In addition, community involvement in reviewing, analyzing, and evaluating the effectiveness of programs from the outset serves to alleviate possible hostilities or the suggestion that certain student groups are being singled out.

The central office must play a key role, supporting programs and practices of a school. Too many school improvement efforts have been thwarted due to halfhearted central office endorsement. "The new adage of top-down support of bottom-up reform efforts must be shown in action, not just in words." (p. 9)

The high school mentioned in this article brought into action all the critical stakeholders in school improvement efforts: community, parents, staff, students, and central office. Such careful planning should serve as a model for other schools in their school improvement efforts.

— Barbara C. Jacoby

CITATION: Morley, Elaine and Shelli B. Rossman, "Cities in Schools: Supporting School Safety Through Services to At-Risk Youth," *Education and Urban Society* 28 (August 1996): 473-491.

What Did the Researchers Do?

What types of services can provide a positive influence on at-risk students with issues such as gang involvement, fighting, and drug and alcohol use? Can safer schools offer an environment conducive to improved attendance, achievement, and attitudes on the part of potential dropouts?

This article examines ways in which programs sponsored by the national, nonprofit Cities in Schools organization address school safety issues affecting at-risk students. Cities in Schools was founded in 1977 to provide local schools with training and technical assistance to reduce the dropout rate and to mitigate related problems affecting at-risk students, such as teen pregnancy, gang involvement, and violence. There are currently 200 community programs in operation; they are typically school-based, autonomous, and self-supporting. Cities in Schools programs initially were established at the high school level, but have been implemented in many middle schools and some elementary schools in recent years.

The Cities in Schools model "is intended to promote more effective provision of services to youths and their families by bringing various agencies together as a team through service coordination and integration at a single site." (p. 475) The organization's name came from this idea of bringing local or "city" services into schools. (p. 475) Case managers, counselors, or mentors are responsible for providing consistent care and support for small groups of at-risk youth.

An analysis of the risk factors affecting 659 students participating in 17 Cities in Schools programs reveals the following demographic characteristics:

- About 85 percent are minorities, primarily African American and Hispanic.

- Forty-eight percent are living in single-parent households.

- Thirty percent exhibit excessive absenteeism.

- Almost 60 percent have repeated at least one grade in school.

- More than one-third were referred to the program because of low academic achievement and poor grades.

Many of the basic components and activities in the Cities in Schools model, primarily intended to reduce the dropout rate, may also facilitate school safety, including:

- Reorganizing a large school into "smaller, more manageable units" or "schools within schools." (p. 481)

- Introducing more humanistic and creative environments, which utilize such strategies as cooperative learning, work-study programs, and peer tutoring.

- Extending school hours to include after-school and summer activities.

- Changing curriculum to address student apathy and alienation, such as adding classes in conflict resolution or violence prevention, law-related courses, and anti-drug or anti-gang sessions.

- Using case managers to establish a positive relationship with students and refer students and their families to available services.

- Increasing involvement of parents and the community.

This article draws on data collected from a multiyear evaluation of Cities in Schools programs. As part of the overall evaluation, a survey was conducted among students in 16 programs to identify the risk factors affecting them and to assess the effectiveness of the program. One-on-one interviews were conducted with 125 students (82 percent in high school) to determine their views of school climate and school safety issues.

What Did the Researchers Find?

Most of the students believe their schools are at least as safe as their home neighborhoods. Some students report considerable levels of violence in their neighborhoods, including regular incidents involving gunshots and drug dealing. These students generally feel their schools are relatively safe. They accept the frequent fights and theft of personal possessions and learn how to survive. In about half of the visited communities, however, Cities in Schools students report that they do not feel safe at school.

Fighting is reported as most prevalent at the beginning of the school year; most fights do not involve weapons because of strong school policies against them. Regular gang activities are not reported as a problem on school premises, though many students have associations with gangs, and, in some cases, are from families whose members have strong links to gangs. Only a few students report drug use in school, but indicate that drug dealing in school is a bigger problem.

Data collected from students who have participated in Cities in Schools programs demonstrate that changes have taken place. Over 69 percent of students participating in the surveys report that the program helped them get along better with other students and over 64 percent believe it helped improve their classroom behavior. Over 31 percent say Cities in Schools helped them reduce drug and alcohol use, and over 70 percent indicate they were less likely to get into trouble with the law. One program in Seattle, Washington increased "individual grade point average (GPA) by at least .5 point if the GPA was below 2.5, and by 1.0 point if the GPA was below 1.0." (p. 487)

Activities that encourage greater involvement between students, parents, and the community at large are key strategies for reducing or avoiding school crime and violence. Diverse approaches include "improving communications with parents so that they are informed of school rules and reinforce such expectations; presenting adult education to enhance parenting skills; collaborating with specialists in criminal justice, juvenile corrections, and mental health arenas who can develop targeted prevention curricula, facilitate early identification of at-risk youth, and provide needed services such as counseling; working with the business sector to develop youth employability skills and after-school or summer jobs for students; modeling prosocial behavior through one-on-one interaction with caring adults; and encouraging students to perform school and community service projects." (p. 482)

Some Cities in Schools programs include police services within the school. The Adopt-a-Cop program recruits volunteers from the police department to interact with students at lunch and on the playground. Another program establishes a gang council which includes security guards, a court administrator, a gang counselor, students, and school personnel. A police partner program uses volunteers from the police department to serve as tutor/mentor/friends to at-risk students.

"Communities that were more successful in obtaining participation from a range of service providers were generally those that had achieved top-down buy-in on the part of school district and other key community leaders. Communities where police and other law enforcement agencies had adopted a prevention orientation, particularly with respect to youth crime and violence, were generally more amenable to placing resources within schools." (p. 489)

What Are Possible Implications for School Improvement?

With the increasing use of alcohol and drugs, and gang activity, many young people could be considered "at risk." Programs like the ones offered through Cities in Schools can help reduce the likelihood of young people becoming involved in such negative activities by enhancing their abilities "to a) bond with peers, family members, and mentors; b) be productive at school, in sports, and in work settings; and c) master various rules and socially accepted routines to improve their life chances." (p. 482)

Although the Cities in Schools "approach is not a panacea, it does offer an additional mechanism not only for meeting the needs of at-risk youth, but also for facilitating additional resources focused on improving the school climate." (p. 490)

— Nancy Berla

EFFECTIVE SCHOOLS RESEARCH ABSTRACTS

SAFE AND ORDERLY ENVIRONMENT

CITATION: Johnson, Patsy E., "Implementing a School-Wide Conflict Management Program: Staff Development is the Key," *Journal of School Leadership* 6, 6 (November 1996): 600-624.

What Did the Researcher Do?

"Schools must develop conflict management programs because much conflict is in our schools—conflict that too frequently takes a destructive course." (p. 600) Many conflict management efforts center around developing, communicating, and enforcing a strong discipline code. Sometimes, these efforts center around the principal becoming a strong (or a stronger) disciplinarian, rather than having the responsibility for desirable student behavior shared by the faculty and the administration.

The underlying philosophy of efforts such as this may be characterized as force against force. Force against force, however, is an ineffective way to deal with the causes of antisocial behavior. Usually "effective" force-against-force programs fade away when the principal leaves. Further, they fail to provide students with positive alternatives to violent patterns of behavior, or to provide the faculty with new knowledge and skills regarding conflict management and prevention.

"The feelings, beliefs, and attitudes found in a school population are as important as its curricular, organizational, and social components." (p. 622) However, changing these dimensions often means overcoming long-term resistance.

How, then, should one proceed? One possible way is provided by this researcher, who reports on an urban middle school's three-year effort to create an intervention program for school conflict that has a "provision for renewal and change." (p. 602)

What Did the Researcher Find?

The wrong way to start a conflict management staff development program is for the principal to announce that it is being instituted in response to a perceived need. Rather, the faculty should be given the opportunity to identify conflict as a school-wide issue. All school staff members have a role in conflict management and "conflict management concepts and principles must permeate the curriculum, activities, and social structure of the school." (p. 602) This is unlikely to happen unless staff considers the program to be a "proactive proposal addressing some well-conceived vision." (p. 603)

Faculty responses to these key questions can provide the information needed to build sustained support for a staff development program: "1. What does the faculty believe regarding the amount and role of conflict in the school? 2. Is the faculty satisfied with the school environment? 3. What are the faculty's perceptions of how their school is viewed by those outside the school, e.g., parents, community, other educators? 4. What behaviors and attitudes reflect faculty acceptance and resistance to planning changes in the school environment to more effectively address conflict issues? 5. What are the faculty's priorities regarding school programs?" (p. 603)

For this study, answers to these questions were gathered through interviews during the school day with each teacher and administrator, through small and large group discussions, and through administering instruments from the National Association of Secondary School Principals' Comprehensive Assessment of School Environments Information Management System. Each person's duties were covered by a substitute during the interview time, to avoid sacrificing planning or break times.

The faculty concluded that they needed staff development before implementing a conflict reduction plan. Comments also indicated that no one had "any unifying idea or experience" to give the school an identity. (p. 608) Further, instead of assuming responsibility for events, the faculty tended to blame others. However, the faculty agreed that it had many strengths that could be drawn upon and developed.

Additional information was gathered from students: "1. What do the students believe regarding the amount and role of conflict in the school? 2. What do the students believe are the causes of conflict in the school? 3. What would the students like to see changed in the school to reduce conflict? 4. How could students change their behavior to reduce conflict? 5. Are the students satisfied with the school environment?" (p. 615) The data-gathering process for the students paralleled the process for the faculty, except that it was gathered from a representative sample of students, instead of the entire student body.

After this thorough information-gathering process, a conflict curriculum was developed for the staff and appropriate instructional materials were selected. The curriculum was built to implement the following:

1. **Presentation of knowledge and theory.** All school personnel must become familiar with the literature on organizational conflict management and the content of the curriculum.

2. **Demonstration of skill—role-play situation.** Role-playing gives participants a chance to exercise new skills. "Modeling different methods and techniques in simulated situations expands the learner's awareness of new possibilities and provides a foil for evaluating current practices." (p. 614)

3. **Protected practice—small group.** "The first opportunity to try new knowledge and develop new skills should be in a nonthreatening environment with no consequences for errors." (p. 614) Small groups of four to six participants can try out different conflict management strategies and discuss possible consequences.

4. **Practice and feedback—individual.** Individuals practice with peers who are not working directly with them. "This practice may be perceived as more threatening, but is still without consequence." (p. 614) Suggestions and feedback from observers can help each participant to improve his or her technique or to apply appropriate knowledge and theories to any given situation.

5. **Coaching.** This stage is a logical extension of the others. A teacher or an administrator is paired with a partner. "They are given opportunities to observe each other in their professional practice environment. Follow-up discussions between the partners focus on the effect that their teaching and management of conflict is having on the students." (p. 614)

The conflict curriculum is based on four standards: "commitment, flexibility, suitability, and innovation." (p. 619) Though "change involving habits, long-held beliefs, expectations, and institutionalized procedures proceeded slowly with resistance," positive progress was still noted early in the program: (p. 620)

- The number of teacher-imposed disciplinary measures, office referrals, and suspensions decreased as the staff became more skilled in conflict management.

- When the teacher and student survey instruments were readministered after 10 to 12 weeks of working with the new conflict curriculum, school satisfaction scores were more positive. "The largest score increase was found for Student Discipline, changing +0.7 standard deviations." (p. 622) Satisfaction scores on all of the other subscales also went up, with the exception of Student Activities.

What Are Possible Implications for School Improvement?

School improvement teams would be well advised to carefully consider and implement the structure reported in this case study. After it was determined, through a process that involved all, that student conflict was a problem, the school improvement team did not rush to adopt a plan. Instead, the team first decided to seek additional data from the faculty and students by asking key questions. The process used to gather and analyze the answers to these questions was thorough and comprehensive. By taking this important step, the school improvement team substantially increased the likelihood that the core issues truly causing the problem would be addressed. A staff development program, which all could agree to, was then designed and implemented.

The staff development program was built upon knowledge of the research, along with demonstration, practice, feedback, and coaching. Staff development programs based upon these elements increase the probability that what is taught will actually be used in the classroom.

— Robert E. Sudlow

EFFECTIVE SCHOOLS RESEARCH ABSTRACTS

SAFE AND ORDERLY ENVIRONMENT

CITATION: Petersen, George J., "Looking at the Big Picture: School Administrators and Violence Reduction," *Journal of School Leadership* 7, 5 (September 1997): 456-479.

What Did the Researcher Do?

Violence or the threat of violence plagues America's public schools in much the same way that it encroaches on the safety of its citizens on the streets. School leaders are faced with the complex challenge of making "schools significantly safer than the streets leading to the schoolhouse door, while maintaining an open atmosphere that emphasizes learning. Not an easy task." (p. 459)

The author had three purposes for this study—1) "to focus on describing the types, frequency, and severity of violence in selected public schools;" 2) "to identify what course of action school administrators in these schools/districts are taking to lessen violence and to focus on the perceived effectiveness of those interventions;" and 3) "to suggest a violence reduction model that administrators could examine and adapt to the particular needs of their schools." (p. 459)

Seventy-seven school administrators, 59 school principals, and 18 district superintendents from 15 school districts of various sizes in 12 states were surveyed to determine their perceptions about school violence. Survey questions were primarily based on a five-point Likert scale interspersed with some forced choice items to test the validity of the instrument and to insure respondents were reading each question and responding appropriately. The final survey was six pages long and contained 162 items.

Domains for the survey questions resulted from a combination of information gained through reviewing past educational literature, as well as recent articles in popular magazines and newspapers. Violence was defined as: "Any form of physical, verbal, or sexual intimidation or aggression that may or may not result in physical harm. This includes traditional forms of conflict (such as fistfighting, swearing, pushing, kicking, etc.) to more extreme forms such as weapons and rape which result in serious or fatal injuries." (p. 461)

What Did the Researcher Find?

Survey results revealed that 25 percent of school administrators were "concerned or very concerned about their personal safety while at school." (p. 469) The greatest concerns "focused on verbal attacks/ threats of violence by the students (12 percent) and/ or the student's parents (14 percent)." (p. 469)

A profile of students who were most frequently victims of violence revealed that they were "males (67.5 percent) from a Caucasian (36 percent) or African American (27 percent) background who were the same age or younger than the perpetrator." (p. 470) Most frequent perpetrators of violent acts "were males (86 percent) from a Caucasian (23 percent), African American (33 percent), or Hispanic (21 percent) background who were the same age or older than the victim." (p. 470)

Survey participants were asked to identify the perceived causes of school violence. Results "suggest that the major elements perceived to contribute to violence in these school districts involved the lack of family involvement and structure, parental violence, and parental drug use." (p. 464)

School administrators were asked to recount the number of actual incidences of violence they had experienced in the last two years to determine whether expressed fears were based on actual experience or due to media influence or rumors. "In the past two years, 57 percent had been verbally threatened or intimidated, 19 percent had been physically threatened or intimidated, and 22 percent of the female administrators had been sexually threatened/harassed or intimidated one or more times." (p. 470) Further, 43 percent said offices and/or school buildings had been seriously vandalized at least once.

Results revealed "that the school environment has 'general areas' where the risk of incidents of school violence are moderately high to very high." (p. 471) These include hallways, restrooms, buses, athletic or extracurricular activities, gymnasiums, and classrooms. "The greatest risk seems to occur during unstructured time when large numbers of students are interacting with one another." (p. 471)

The most commonly implemented programs for violence reduction in the schools included (in order): poverty issue programs (such as breakfast programs); stricter, uniform approach to discipline; visitor registration; peer mediation/conflict resolution; alternative schools or educational models; business/school partnerships; programs to increase parent involvement; the presence of teachers in hallways; dress codes; before- and after-school programs; and conflict management training programs for teachers. (p. 471)

The top five programs most commonly ranked as effective were teachers present in hallways, stricter discipline policies, security personnel, peer mediation/conflict resolution training, and poverty issue programs. (p. 468) The five listed most often as least effective were social skills training, dress codes, parental involvement programs, business/school partnerships, and, again, stricter discipline policies. (p. 469)

What Are Possible Implications for School Improvement?

The author proposes a model for school violence prevention which includes five major components targeted to preschool and elementary children. "The need for intervention at the preschool/elementary level is essential because interventions targeting middle schools and high schools have met with limited success." (p. 473) Research indicates that "prevention models focused on at-risk populations have been shown to be effective when implemented at the preschool/elementary level." (p. 474) This model consists of the following elements:

Family inclusion. Restructuring schools to make them function as "town centers" to support, include, and engage the entire family in the scope of the educational setting is essential. (p. 474)

Evolution of teacher/administrator roles. In addition to its primary focus on student academic development, schools will need to fill the gap in the development of students' ethical and moral behavior if families are unable or unwilling to become involved. Teachers and administrators, especially at the preschool/elementary level, will need to be trained in delivering a comprehensive values education.

Student success. Creating a school atmosphere that helps "engender self-esteem by encouraging individual pride and creating a sense of student ownership" can serve as a deterrent to violent acts. (p. 475) "The need to establish the appropriate emotional environment, build self-esteem, and establish a democratic school structure are essential elements in assuring student success." (p. 476)

Conflict mediation. While not recommending a specific mediation program, "this component emphasizes that the teaching of some form of conflict mediation, negotiation procedures, and constructive resolution skills should be included in the curriculum of every classroom." (p. 476) Collective leadership by teachers and administrators must be focused "on teaching children the value of cooperating, sharing, and helping others." (p. 476)

Media intervention. In order to combat the unrelenting influence of media violence, schools must teach visual literacy in addition to print literacy. To help deal with the influences children are exposed to outside of school, educators can use strategies such as creating a safe classroom atmosphere, presenting reading material that covers personal and ethical issues, and involving parents in discussions on family choices for viewing, listening, and reading. Children must be taught to critically evaluate the violence they see on the screen and learn to evaluate its impact on their own lives.

— Judy Wilson Stevens

CITATION: Kratzer, Cindy C., "Roscoe Elementary School: Cultivating a Caring Community in an Urban Elementary School," *Journal of Education for Students Placed At Risk* 2, 4 (1997): 345-375.

What Did the Researcher Do?

"The cultivation of a caring community within an urban neighborhood public elementary school is viewed by some educators as an impossibility, by others as being in conflict with academic effectiveness, and by still others as unnecessary for the successful achievement of students. Nevertheless, a significant group of educators advocate schools as caring communities, particularly in meeting the needs of low-income urban students of color." (p. 345)

The researcher conducted a single-site case study during one school year to examine how one urban public school demonstrated characteristics of a caring community. Using case study methodology, the researcher "examined what it meant to insiders and onlookers for a school to exhibit community, the process of cultivating a caring community, and the larger context in which this process took place." (p. 349)

The selection of the school for the study was based on recommendations from others who were working with urban schools involved in reform efforts. Achievement criteria were also used, and though the school's achievement was not exemplary, it was better than that of other local public schools serving students with similar backgrounds. The school had a reputation for curricular and instructional innovation and for successful implementation of site-based management principles.

Primary data collection consisted of almost 250 hours of observation of classrooms, school activities, parent meetings, faculty and governance council meetings, as well as audiotaped interviews with students, parents, teachers, and administrators. Classroom documents were collected to examine the historical and social context of the site; field notes were also reviewed.

Roscoe Elementary School, 16 miles from downtown Los Angeles, is part of the Los Angeles Unified School District, the nation's second largest. Most area residents are blue-collar workers or unskilled laborers. There are many Latin American, Southeast Asian, and Middle Eastern emigrants moving in and out of the area. The percentage of Hispanic students is 92.6 percent, African-American and Filipino are each about 2 percent, and white students 3 percent. The school is large; its student body grew from 797 in 1991 to 1,170 students by 1996. Of these, 90 percent were eligible for Title I services, 76 percent were Limited English Proficient (LEP), and 95 percent were eligible for free or reduced lunch. Because of overcrowding, the school operated on a year-round schedule. Each of the 39 classes had a part-time aide.

What Did the Researcher Find?

1. Prevailing Themes of Caring and Community

Roscoe School had many characteristics that could make a strong, caring community unlikely. It was a large school that had to operate on a year-round schedule; students and teachers were never all in the building at the same time. Its students came from a low socioeconomic level and from a variety of ethnic and linguistic backgrounds. Nevertheless, Roscoe did evidence a strong, caring community. The researcher attributed that phenomenon to three central "themes," which were the foundation of the school's success:

Climate of mutual respect and trust. At Roscoe, teachers demonstrated collegiality and collaboration and readily shared educational ideas. There was significant evidence of trust and respect among teachers, administrators, and parents. Administrators supported teacher decision-making in instructional areas. Parents expressed feelings of being welcome at the school and felt they were listened to when they had concerns. Although there was often a wide range of opinions on how to accomplish goals, "the school fostered an environment in which it was safe and legitimate to express an opinion, even if that opinion was not widely shared." (p. 353)

Fluid boundaries around an ethic of caring. The school evidenced an atmosphere where "formal roles and structures were less critical and influential than were relationships and informal interactions." (p. 354) Teachers and administrators went beyond the stated requirements of their roles in ways that promoted an attitude of caring. In the classrooms, an atmosphere of "warmth, enthusiasm, and creativity" prevailed. (p. 355) Students commonly helped each other with learning tasks, and there were few behavior conflicts among students. The staff also exhibited a strong ethic of caring toward parents.

Collective and individual sense of ownership and responsibility. This was evident in the principal's ability to delegate appropriate responsibilities to staff members and to praise them for taking these on. Teachers also demonstrated willingness to take initiative. At all levels, caring for the school was an ongoing theme. Parents were encouraged to become involved and to initiate a variety of activities. "There was also a strong perception at the school that everyone had a responsibility to care for all the children, not just those in their classroom." (p. 357)

2. Community and Restructuring

The institution of site-based management and shared decision making allowed the school to control its budget, and the hiring and termination of employees; adjust its calendar and day-to-day schedules; solicit external funding sources; adopt its own textbooks; and provide staff development centered on its needs and goals. Other structural mechanisms promoted community for students, including a wide variety of student leadership opportunities. Parent involvement structures (weekly parent education meetings, a community representative who acted as liaison to parents, and the renovation of the Parent Center) also promoted a sense of community.

3. Community and Achievement

Achievement seen in the context of total student growth. Roscoe school staff embraced a mission which supported both student learning and student development. Achievement was regarded as one means to personal growth and development. The staff wanted students to be excited about learning. The staff did not believe that standardized, norm-referenced tests were adequate measures of student learning, but they also knew that the students would need to be able to do well on such assessments throughout their lives. Staff was continually working to improve the quality of instruction in a larger context than standardized norm-referenced assessments. This effort included reflective dialogue that centered on student learning, awareness of educational research, and an interdisciplinary curriculum.

Link between the individual and the whole. The well-being of individuals in the school was inseparable from the well-being of the school as a whole. "When teachers have embraced this connection, they will not be satisfied until the school is good enough for their own children to attend, which is exactly what happened at Roscoe." (p. 365)

Integrating affective concerns. At Roscoe, effectiveness included the affective domain. Staff "examined not only test scores and attendance rates, but also the relationships, ideology, and motivations of people in the school." (p. 366) Teacher and student interactions reflected a sense of mutual respect, dignity, trust, and fairness.

4. The Process of Cultivating Community

The cultivation of a climate of community and effectiveness at Roscoe School was due to a combination of factors: "careful hiring of teachers, positive instructional leadership along with appropriate delegation of authority, timely response to felt needs, ongoing reflective dialogue about student learning and pedagogy, and an academic press that continually sought to improve." (p. 373) Thus, factors were cultivated within "a culture that fostered trust, caring, and ownership and a structure that enabled such values to thrive." (p. 372)

What Are Possible Implications for School Improvement?

Effectiveness in both the social-emotional and the academic domains is important for school improvement that centers on the whole person. A positive school climate is a key characteristic of schools that are effective for all children. This case study once again reinforces previous research that the establishment of a caring school community is an important factor in a school's ability to make a difference in the lives of children. This includes urban students living in lower socioeconomic neighborhoods and those who come from diverse ethnic and linguistic backgrounds. In fact, for these children, more than any others, a supportive school culture may be the crucial factor which makes school success possible.

— Lynn Benore

EFFECTIVE SCHOOLS RESEARCH ABSTRACTS

SAFE AND ORDERLY ENVIRONMENT

CITATION: Murray, Richard K., "The Impact of School Uniforms on School Climate," *NASSP Bulletin* 81, 593 (December 1997): 106-112.

What Did the Researcher Do?

Many educators firmly believe that school uniforms have a positive effect on school climate. But does the research back this up?

The author, a principal of a high school in South Carolina, was interested in testing this hypothesis. He notes that, prior to his study in the spring of 1996, "no true research had been conducted to determine the effects of school uniforms on school climate. Despite this lack of research, school districts across the country have implemented school uniforms hoping to improve student attendance, maintain student discipline, ensure student achievement, promote student self-esteem, and enhance school climate." (p. 106)

In his study, Murray administered the National Association of Secondary School Principals' School Climate Survey to 306 sixth, seventh, and eighth graders from two similar urban middle schools. One school had a school uniform policy; the other did not. In other respects—racial composition and numbers of students receiving free/reduced price lunch—the schools were almost identical. Both drew students from the same urban area.

The survey administered to these students included such statements as:

- *Students usually feel safe in the school building.*

- *Students here understand why they are in school.*

- *Students in this school are well-behaved even when the teachers are not watching them.* (p. 107)

The 55 statements on the survey are divided into 10 subscales: teacher-student relationships; security and maintenance; administration; student academic orientation; student behavioral values; guidance; student-peer relationships; parent and community school relationships; instructional management; and student activities.

What Did the Researcher Find?

Students at the school with the uniform policy (School A) rated their school climate more positively than did the students in the non-uniform school (School B). In nine of the 10 subscales, students in School A rated their school climate more positively than students in School B. The researcher found that these differences were significant in seven of the subscales—teacher-student relationships; security and maintenance; student behavioral values; guidance; parent and community school relations; instructional management; and student activities.

Students in School A indicated stronger, more positive relationships with their teachers. Survey questions included statements such as: *Teachers in this school like their students. Teachers help students to be friendly and kind to each other. Teachers treat each student as an individual. Teachers are fair to students.* (p. 108)

Asked how they felt about security and maintenance at their school, a significantly higher number of students in School A indicated that students, teachers, and other workers feel safe in the building before and after school, and that people are not afraid to come to school for evening events. Such perceptions were found in the total school responses and among grade levels.

The responses of students in School A on the subscale of guidance were significantly higher than those in School B. This subscale included such statements as: *Teachers or counselors help students with personal problems. Students in this school can get help and advice from teachers or counselors. Teachers or counselors encourage students to think about their future. Teachers and counselors help students plan for future classes and for future jobs.* (p. 109)

Students in School A also had significantly higher ratings on the subscale related to instructional management, which included such areas as the efficiency and effectiveness of teacher classroom organization and the use of classroom time.

School B did have a higher mean than School A in administration. "This section contained questions designed to produce responses concerning the degree to which school administrators are effective in communicating with different role groups and in setting high performance expectations for the teachers and students. Although School B had the higher mean, results were not significant." (p. 108) There were no significant differences between the two schools in student academic orientation and student-peer relationships.

The researcher also compared the survey responses of the students in the two schools to national norms. "When contrasted with national norms, School A compared rather closely, with higher mean scores in the teacher-student relationships and guidance subscales and an identical score in the student behavioral values subscale." (p. 108) School B, on the other hand, "did not compare well against the national norms, with lower mean scores in all 10 subscales." (p. 108)

What Are Possible Implications for School Improvement?

The adoption of school uniforms has long been advocated by some school administrators as an effective means of improving school climate and student behavior, and the findings of this study would seem to give credence to this. According to the researcher, it is the first study to find a relationship between school climate and school uniforms. (p. 110) School uniforms have a significant impact on school climate and school climate "has been shown to be related to student achievement, as well as how students behave and feel about themselves, their school, and other individuals." (p. 110)

Administrators considering implementation of school uniforms will find this study contains the data they need to convince others. And administrators who have opposed school uniforms may well reconsider their standing after learning about the findings in this study.

School uniforms "will not solve all problems associated with today's schools. However, school uniforms now appear to have benefits such as improving students' perceptions of school climate." (p. 111) Administrators concerned with the improvement of school climate would do well to pay heed to this research.

— Kate O'Neill

EFFECTIVE SCHOOLS RESEARCH ABSTRACTS

SAFE AND ORDERLY ENVIRONMENT

CITATION: Daniel, R.E., "The Student Leadership Institute," *Students Taking the Lead: The Challenges and Rewards of Empowering Youth in Schools.* New Directions for School Leadership 4, Jossey-Bass, San Francisco, CA, Summer 1997.

What Did the Researcher Do?

This chapter from a book on student leadership describes one North Carolina high school's reform effort that led to the establishment of the Student Leadership Institute to meet a "critical need for student ownership in the school." (p. 27) The mission of the Institute was to identify and develop positive leadership potential among members of the student body.

At one time, this school was regarded with high esteem, but over the years and due to numerous circumstances, it became the object of tension and dissatisfaction within its own community. After a series of conversations, the principal and students began building on an idea generated by the students themselves: the students would be placed in "leadership and decision-making positions with real input and influence over school policy and practices." (p. 29)

In developing the initial idea into a full-grown program, the principal enlisted the help of two teachers. They decided to concentrate on actual leadership practices and look past the obvious school-centered indicators. Sometimes "the 'true' leaders are not the ones we wish they would be; often students pick their own leaders for reasons other than strong character, a sense of honor, or super achievement. So, for us there was no minimum grade average, no specific attendance or performance criteria, no teacher recommendations, no grade-level quota." (pp. 29-30) The Institute was open to any student who nominated himself or herself and was willing to commit to training.

The training process was modeled after civic leadership training programs in various cities and states. The first weekend training retreat was attended by 41 students, including elected student leaders, athletes, class clowns, cheerleaders, "geeky nerds," and "some pregrunge longhairs." (p. 30) The group was predominantly white and female. Five years later, the group remains predominately female, but the racial mix has changed to reflect the 50-50 school population.

Ongoing training consists of one to two days each month in seminars and workshops designed to introduce students to their city and country with unique economic, political, historical, and educational challenges. The students take field trips and participate in forums and other events in which civic, legal, and business leaders are brought into the school.

What Did the Researcher Find?

The first group of students took on, as its first project, the challenge of improving race relations at the high school. As the principal stated, "the students rose to the occasion brilliantly, without our help except in 'greasing the skids' for logistical support." (p. 32) By the end of the year, race relations had improved remarkably as the students worked diligently within the community, as well as in the school setting.

Additional projects involved efforts to improve scholarships through volunteer tutoring, a focus on academics, and a specific effort to back up the teacher in establishing an enthusiastic atmosphere for learning.

The public image of the school began to change as students and community leaders took the initiative to "talk up" the school. (p. 33) Students and parents are "no longer afraid to challenge people they overhear in the grocery line and other public places who are spreading damaging falsehoods about the school (a prevalent practice until recently)." (pp. 33-34)

Over the last five years, the Institute has grown from a small group of students willing to buck the tide of tradition into a well-organized group of conscientious students who take their role very seriously. In addition to giving up numerous hours in seminars, forums, retreats, field trips, and study sessions, they demand the highest level of behavior from themselves.

Empowerment of students to intervene in their own learning environment can be remarkably successful. It is possible to create a high school culture where student leaders, acting in concert with the faculty, staff, and administration, work to achieve goals for the good of the entire community.

Even in the best of programs, though, "there will always be a few people who fall short of the program's expectations." (p. 35) From the outset, members of the Institute were considered "the principal's pets" by some faculty and staff members. (p. 35) The principal anticipated how the faculty might respond to these students and built a method of dealing with this into training sessions. It was critical to show that Institute training and participation "could and would change these students' attitudes, so that they could overcome this history with the faculty and staff." (p. 35)

What Are Possible Implications for School Improvement?

The author concludes with a summary of advice for building principals who are considering starting an organization similar to the Student Leadership Institute:

- Be serious. Students are adept at spotting phonies; mean what you say.

- Recognize the students' right to ownership. Students must take charge of their own efforts.

- Back students up. The effort will fail if students do not have the authority to effect real change. This is a powerful argument for having the principal act as chief advisor. The school faculty, staff, and administration must be willing to give students the opportunity to try and to fail without crushing their enthusiasm.

- "Expect the students to rise to the occasion." (p. 37) Believe that students will act responsibly and give them full authority to do so. Show by your actions that you trust and support their efforts.

- "Maintain high standards." (p. 37) Expect all students to exhibit constant leadership behavior in school and in the community. Though they are trained in the "subtle art of peer pressure manipulation," do not "impose on them the burden of being 'student administrators.'" (p. 38) Insist that they exercise their own leadership judgment and stop any detrimental behavior.

- Know the difference between "advisor" and "leader." (p. 38) Students choose their leaders; the principal is the chief advisor.

- "Give no slack." (p. 38) Take the necessary action if an Institute student forgets the training and becomes involved in irresponsible behavior. Institute students must believe that they are held to the same expectations as others and will be shown no favoritism. In fact, they should be well aware that they are held to a higher level of responsibility and will not "get away" with anything simply because of their membership.

- Some of the most serious and effective student leaders may not be the most outstanding scholars. Be willing to recognize student leadership potential among the whole student body.

- This project is "ongoing and must be constantly attended to." (p. 39) Every four years, there is a new group of students who will need to learn about the program.

As this principals puts it, "if you have never seen highly trained and highly motivated determined teenagers tackle a problem with no thought of defeat, you have never seen one of the most beautiful and inspiring sights an educator can ever see. For these are truly the citizens under whose leadership you and I will pass the torch of power and civilization to a new generation." (p. 36)

— Barbara C. Jacoby

CITATION: McPartland, James, Robert Balfanz, Will Jordan, and Nettie Legters, "Improving Climate and Achievement in a Troubled Urban High School Through the Talent Development Model," *Journal of Education for Students Placed At Risk* 3, 4 (1998): 337-361.

What Did the Researchers Do?

Patterson High School in Baltimore, Maryland was one of the first schools to be given a mandate to improve by the state. If it did not improve, it would face a state takeover.

At the time of the mandate (1994), Patterson was identified as one of the two worst high schools in Maryland. The school climate was unsafe, chaotic, and not conducive to learning. On any given day, approximately 40 percent of students were absent. Natural byproducts of this were low achievement and high dropout rates.

Patterson responded to the threatened takeover by hiring a new principal and teaming up with the Center for Research on the Education of Students Placed At Risk, a federally funded research team at Johns Hopkins and Howard Universities. Working together, the planning team identified three challenges.

The first challenge was the size of the school and the anonymity which accompanied it. "Teachers and administrators did not know the names of many of the students whom they passed in the halls and corridors, and anonymous students felt secure in disregarding directions or verbally abusing adults." (p. 339) The response to this challenge was to divide the school into five Academies. Each Academy was a small school-within-a-school where teachers, students, and administrators could get to know one another and learn to respect others. Academies have separate sections of the building, each with its own unique entrance, faculty, administrators, guidance counselors, and custodial staff. Additionally, classes were extended to 90 minutes each, eliminating two transition periods and reducing the possibility of disciplinary problems between classes and class cutting.

Student apathy about school (they saw little connection between school and their outside interests and goals) was the second challenge identified. To overcome this, the planning team chose to provide a career focus for four of the Academies. The four Career Academies were for sophomores, juniors, and seniors only and focused on Arts and Humanities; Business and Finance; Sports Studies and Health/Wellness; and Transportation and Engineering Technology. Each Career Academy provided students with basic academic courses, career-focused electives, and internship opportunities.

The final challenge identified was the fact that freshmen entered with a wide range of preparation in the basic academic subjects, yet all freshmen were required to take a core curriculum of college preparatory material. To help all students succeed, the planning team created the Ninth Grade Success Academy and the Twilight School.

The Ninth Grade Success Academy provided a transition from middle school to high school and was structured around small interdisciplinary teams of four to five teachers. Each team had the same students and a common planning time, fostering the development of positive relationships between students and staff and helping teachers find solutions to student attendance, discipline, and learning problems. Additionally, this Academy provided extra time and resources to students who were having difficulty with the core courses, offered extensive self-awareness opportunities concerning career goals and interests, and gave students detailed information on high school choices and college alternatives.

The Twilight School was an alternative program for students with serious discipline or attendance problems or students who were coming to Patterson from prison or from expulsion from another school. Classes were taught in small groups after school hours and extensive support was provided for each student. The goal was to provide students with the necessary academic, social, and emotional skills so they could reenter regular day school and be successful there.

It took a year for Patterson faculty to identify these challenges and create solutions. The goal for the first year of implementation "was to provide a clear sense of safety and seriousness and to give students a focus for their studies so they would attend regularly and see meaning in their program of courses." (p. 344) Planning time came from regularly scheduled staff development days and from time volunteered before and after school. All of this work fostered a sense of ownership in the Academies and a commitment to success.

What Did the Researchers Find?

Researchers found evidence, both qualitative and quantitative, of significant improvement at the new Talent Development School with Career Academies. The qualitative indicators were visible from the beginning of the 1995-1996 school year. Students were cheerfully greeted each day by teachers and administrators who knew their names. Halls were clear during class time and teachers now taught with their doors wide open. Rules were enforced by teachers and administrators and followed by students. Teachers personally phoned students when they were absent, letting students know they cared about them coming to school. By the second year of implementation, there was one security officer at the school as opposed to up to seven prior to implementation.

Between 1993-1994 (the year in which Patterson was identified) and 1996-1997 (the second implementation year), total school attendance rose 10.1 percent (to 78.9 percent) and attendance in the freshmen class rose 15.5 percent (to 77.4 percent). Additionally, the number of students who missed 20 or more days of school decreased by 10 percent.

Promotion of students from one grade to the next improved. At the end of the first and second implementation years, approximately 15 percent of the freshman class was held back compared with over 50 percent prior to implementation. Also, the number of upperclassmen grew by almost 66 percent.

Student achievement, measured by the percent passing state functional tests, also improved. Between 1994 and 1997, students passing the

mathematics test increased 28 percent, giving Patterson the highest pass rate of the nine high schools in the Baltimore City School District. Patterson also achieved the third highest pass rate on the state writing exam.

Maryland uses a school performance index to rate and compare its schools, based on student attendance, retention, and test scores. In 1995, Patterson was ranked eighth out of the nine Baltimore City High Schools according to this index. By 1997, Patterson moved up to second, and this progress occurred during a period of stagnation for most of the other schools.

In a survey before and after the implementation, teachers were asked to rate serious problems at their school. In every single category, the percent of teachers rating a problem as serious decreased. The most significant decreases were absenteeism, class cutting, tardiness, and vandalism. Finally, students share in the perception of improved school climate. In a survey which compares Patterson students' perception of their school with student perceptions in a comparable school, Patterson scored higher in every instance.

What Are Possible Implications for School Improvement?

The case study of Patterson High School clearly shows how an improved school climate affects achievement in a positive manner.

Replication of the Talent Development Model with Career Academies has already been attempted at four other Baltimore schools. While not yet 100 percent successful at the new sites, the researchers have learned some important lessons. School faculty and administration must be involved in planning adaptations and implementation so they will buy in to the reform efforts. Also, scheduling problems must be solved so different Academies can remain separate physically and have unique identities. The school-wide principal must understand and support the model, and be willing to delegate leadership and responsibility to Academy principals.

"The challenge now is to bootstrap these improvements into even higher levels of performance and to transmit the same Talent Development Model with support systems to other high schools that seek to turn themselves around." (p. 360)

— Martha S. Osterhaudt

EFFECTIVE SCHOOLS RESEARCH ABSTRACTS

SAFE AND ORDERLY ENVIRONMENT

CITATION: Rasicot, Julie, "The Threat of Harm," Busse, Nancy, "I Can't Keep Them Safe!", and Haynes, Richard M. and Donald M. Chalker, "A Nation of Violence," *The American School Board Journal* 186, 3 (March 1999): 14-25.

What Did the Researchers Do?

Concern for the safety of students in America's schools has moved the effective schools correlate of creating a safe and orderly environment to the top of the list for school leaders. Recent examples of shootings in districts across the nation have resulted in a sharpened focus on causes of school violence and greatly increased the list of suggestions for reducing the possibility for further outbreaks. In this issue of *The American School Board Journal*, two articles focus on schools that have successfully handled violent incidents and one article looks at how American schools compare to those in other developed nations on the issue of school violence.

In "The Threat of Harm," Jose Martinez, principal of a high school in Burlington, Wisconsin, shares the frightening experience of discovering a plot by five students to take over the school and use student records to find students they wanted to harm. If innocent students or others got in their way, they planned to kill them. Although the principal found it hard to believe the five students had really intended such a vicious act, after the accused students confessed their plot to police, Martinez had to accept the reality of their intent.

Events such as this have resulted in the development of tougher policies regarding threats to harm students or school personnel. Questions have arisen about how to discipline a student who has made such a threat. Many districts have instituted a zero tolerance policy and do not attempt to differentiate between pranks or words spoken in anger. All threats are treated as real and severe punishment follows.

Some critics of the strict school policies have urged district officials to follow "a more deliberative approach that explores a student's motives and metes out

punishment on an individual basis." (p. 16) Citing a case in which a student was expelled for using gun photos and rap song lyrics in a creative writing assignment, the American Civil Liberties Union (ACLU) intervened and the student was returned to school. The suspension was removed from his record.

In "I Can't Keep Them Safe!", Nancy Busse, then dean of students at Le Sueur-Henderson High School in Le Sueur, Minnesota, recounts the difficult experience of an actual shooting by a student in her school. Some students gave early warning about the threats made by this troubled 16 year-old student, but despite increased security and protection from the local police, the troubled student was able to penetrate the confines of the school with a gun. Quick thinking by a school janitor and brave action by a police officer resulted in the student's capture with only the arresting officer receiving a superficial wound to the head. When the student's car was searched, police found "a stolen assault weapon, with 130 rounds of ammunition." (p. 21)

What Did the Researchers Find?

In both of these cases, school officials had to deal with reacting to potential threats prior to the actual performance of violent acts. In "The Threat of Harm," the author offers examples of school boards adopting policies with significant consequences for students accused of "making terroristic threats or committing such acts." (p. 16) In addition to expulsion, convicted students may be unable to return to the school until officials find "competent and credible evidence that the student does not pose a risk of harm to others." (p. 17) Students who have been expelled may also be subject to random searches once they return to school. Staff and students are also expected to alert the principal if they become aware of a possible threatening act. Members of the ACLU are concerned that students' rights will be violated as school officials increase the vigorous pursuit of potentially violent students. "This kind of policy can lead to not distinguishing what's real or what's a kid's fantasy or joke." (p. 17)

The author recommends using an early warning guide developed by the U.S. Departments of Education and Justice to help determine if a student represents a serious threat or has the potential for violence. The guide suggests training a team of adults who can make decisions about the seriousness of the behavior of students making threats. It also stresses the importance of providing training for the staff in recognizing early warning signs of potential violent behavior, including "uncontrolled anger, social withdrawal, excessive feelings of rejection, and feelings of being picked on and persecuted." (p. 17)

Busse, in her article, recommends developing a school culture grounded in the principles of "judicious discipline," a management style based on "the synthesis of professional ethics, good educational practice, and students' constitutional rights." (p. 21) Busse credits the creation of a school culture based on trust and the development of a sense of responsibility to protect their school with giving the troubled student's friends the courage to share information with authorities about the violent acts being planned.

In the third feature article in the series, "A Nation of Violence" by Richard M. Haynes and Donald M. Chalker, the authors offer grim statistics about the safety of American schools when compared to those of other developed nations. Their findings, along with suggestions for improvement, offer significant possibilities for increasing safety for the nation's students. Research by these professors from Western Carolina University indicates that the United States leads the developed world when it comes to violence among young people. Nearly 5,300 children died as a result of firearms in 1995, averaging nearly 30 children each day in a school year and representing a full 87 percent of all violent deaths among children aged 5 to 15 in 26 developed nations. (p. 22) "The United States is also a world leader in another violence indicator: the number of young people who take their own lives." (p. 22) Many of the students who take their own lives do so with guns.

Though violent acts are perpetrated in other countries, the authors believe that "school-aged children in the United States are learning a lesson glorifying violence, a lesson seldom taught in other developed nations." (p. 23) In the U.S., infants have a homicide rate that "is 177 percent that of infants in other countries. The rate of suspected child abuse in that age group is 208 percent more than the world average." (p. 22) The authors conclude that something is "clearly wrong in American culture." (p. 22)

What Are Possible Implications for School Improvement?

Haynes and Chalker offer these suggestions for reducing violence in U.S. schools:

Control handguns. Most European nations have strict handgun controls. Japan bans gun ownership by anyone other than the military and has near zero deaths among school-aged children. Even in countries like Canada, where hunting is popular, there are no handguns.

Put a stop to television violence. Many countries are attempting to decrease violence on television. One way to reduce children's exposure to violence is to limit the amount of television watched. The authors recommend that children not be allowed to watch unsupervised television or have unlimited access to the Internet behind closed doors.

Isolate violent students. In other countries, students who exhibit violent tendencies are sent to special education schools where they are isolated from others. Another idea that may be worth copying is Singapore's policy of deputizing administrators and teachers as "honorary police officers" who are trained in physical restraint and juvenile law, and have full powers of arrest. (p. 24)

Schools are not the cause of student violence, but they must operate in a society in which such violence is prevalent. School boards are asked to seriously consider policies that will focus on strategies that increase educators' knowledge about symptoms of troubled youth, how to handle threats, and how to create school cultures in which everyone feels responsible for keeping the school safe and secure.

— Judy Wilson Stevens

Section II

Physical Plant

of the School

Physical Plant
of the School

It appears that school size and building condition can have very real and direct impacts on student behavior.

- When small schools are consolidated into megaschools, the quality of the school environment tends to suffer.

- Breakdowns in communication and less staff involvement in decision making occur more frequently in large schools than in smaller schools.

- Positive student attitudes decrease delinquent behavior in schools of all sizes, but the effect is even greater in large schools.

- The larger the school, the greater the program diversity, but the less positive the social climate. Further, social climate has a stronger influence on dropout rates than program diversity.

- Diversity in academics is more important to keeping students in school and motivated than is diversity in facilities.

- Dividing large schools into smaller subschools creates a more stable, intimate, supportive environment.

- Parental involvement has an impact on school building conditions. In turn, building conditions have a significant impact on student achievement.

- Safe and well-maintained schools are important influences on student attitudes and achievement. Though violence certainly can and does happen in comfortable, pleasing surroundings, a poorly maintained school building gives a message to students that nobody cares about their school. If the adults don't care, why should they?

In summary, smaller schools (or schools-within-a-school) and well-maintained facilities appear to encourage collective responsibility for student success and a decrease in disruptive behavior.

EFFECTIVE SCHOOLS RESEARCH ABSTRACTS

SAFE AND ORDERLY ENVIRONMENT

CITATION: Gottfredson, Denise C., *School Size and School Disorder.* Baltimore, MD: Johns Hopkins University, Center for Social Organization of Schools. Report No. 360, July 1985. Funded in part by the National Institute of Education, U.S. Department of Education (NIE-G-830002).

What Did the Researcher Do?

A timely research topic, school disorder, is characterized in this report as disruptions such as student and teacher victimization, unsafe school climates for both teachers and students, serious student delinquency, and student drug involvement. Gottfredson saw the need to examine the effects of school size on school disorder, because 1) policymakers need information about the effects on school climate and student psychological and academic functioning, and 2) educational leaders need to study school-size influences to help manipulate environments that can mediate learning structures advantageous to school learning regardless of school size.

The population studied were 42 of 69 schools in 17 cities including urban, smaller city and town, U.S. Territories, and rural Indian reservation schools that participated in a national survey.[1] The study included random samples from grades 6-12, since the issue of school disruption is "most central to secondary schools." (p. 12)

The research encompassed prior work by Gottfredson and others around two topics: school administration and student participation. The relation of school size to school disorder was the primary issue around which they developed hypotheses.

School administration. Related research reports that school governance policies and procedures are important determinants of the level of school disorder. Large schools make it harder for the administration to respond to misbehavior; often students are unsupervised or lost in the shuffle. Large schools with strict rules can seem impersonal. Because of the perception of impersonality, staff morale can become low, precluding faculty from thinking of innovative ways to solve problems.

Student participation. Research concerning students' marginality (rated by academic success, self concept, attachment to school, social integration, and interpersonal competency) were among theoretical variables used to discuss students' participation in extracurricular activities as a deterrent to disruptive or delinquent school behavior.

What Did the Researcher Find?

Selected discussions from the study of the effects of school size on school disorder include:

- School size is related to school safety and to teachers' perceptions of school administrations' and faculties' general morale. There is "some support for the notion that school disorder results from poor school administration." (p. 41) In large schools, a breakdown occurs in communication, feedback about performance, and staff involvement in decision making. "Teachers in these schools lose confidence in the administration and feel ineffective. Disorder results." (p. 41)

- "Positive student attitudes decrease delinquent behavior for students in schools of all sizes, but the effect is largest in large schools." (p. 39)

- Involvement is particularly important for students who lack academic routes to success (marginal students).

- "Differences on delinquency, attachment to school, and participation for students in schools of different sizes is more marked for marginal students than for others." (p. 35)

- "Marginal females in large schools, for example, report using more than twice as many different kinds of drugs as do marginal students in small schools." (p. 32)

- In case studies where a dramatic change in school size was used as a variable, an interesting outcome was reported. Some schools that either increased or decreased in size began to experience disorder. Reasons and situations varied and were illuminated. (The reader is encouraged to refer to the source article for further discussion.)

What Are Possible Implications for School Improvement?

In schools working to become more effective, policy-makers and school leaders need to pay attention to variables which can ameliorate any negative results that might evolve from the effects of either a particularly large or small school size. Staff should especially monitor those schools experiencing rapid changes in enrollment.

Effective schools researchers verify that teaching and learning in schools thrive in a safe and orderly environment where frequent monitoring of outcomes, strong instructional leadership, focused mission on student outcomes, and high expectations for students and staff are present.

The study in its entirety offered incisive interpretations around the variables discussed here. School leaders and faculty must pay attention to the ramifications of school size, whether small or large, and the changing size of their schools in order to assure the promotion of more effective environments for teaching and learning. It appears that smooth administration of schools is a significant promoter of staff morale and, ultimately, positive student learning and behavior.

— Beverly A. Bancroft

---

[1] School Action Effectiveness Study data was originally collected for a much larger study as part of a national evaluation by the Office of Juvenile Justice and Delinquency Prevention Alternative Education Initiative (G. Gottfredson, 1982.) Surveys of students and teachers were conducted in the spring of 1982.

CITATION: Pittman, Robert B. and Perri Haughwout, "Influence of High School Size on Dropout Rate," *Educational Evaluation and Policy Analysis* 9, 4 (Winter 1987): 337-343.

What Did the Researchers Do?

School consolidation and student dropouts are two issues which frequently must be dealt with by school boards. Yet the possibility that there may be a link between the two is almost never considered. This study was designed to assess the relative effect of school size on characteristics that could potentially link school size and dropout rate. Those factors which have been identified in the literature include school opportunity, level of participation, overall satisfaction with school, and the quality of the school environment. Thus, the researchers sought to answer the question: "Does school size influence dropout rate, independent of the overall climate of the school, or is its impact totally indirect, through the general school climate?" (p. 337)

The theoretical base of this study rested on the prevailing attitude of the last 30 years, that consolidating smaller schools into larger units offered students greater academic opportunity and was more economical. (Conant, 1959) More recently, other researchers have concluded that, although large schools do have more curricular and extracurricular offerings, students who attend small schools participate in more activities and receive a greater diversity of experience. (Campbell et al., 1981)

This study used information from 988 public, comprehensive high schools that participated in the High School and Beyond study of the National Center of Educational Statistics. This longitudinal study investigated high school students during the spring of 1980. A random sample of 36 seniors and 36 sophomores from the respective class populations at the participating schools completed a battery of tests and a 120-item questionnaire. The questions focused on various characteristics of the school and the student population. Principals or other administrators of the selected schools also responded to a 68-item questionnaire. The study assessed four major school variables: dropout rate, climate, program diversity, and size. Various regression equations were used to analyze the data.

What Did the Researchers Find?

The first phase of the study described the magnitude of the relationship between school size and dropout rate. Based on the correlation coefficiencies, increasing the size of the student body corresponded to a similar rise in the school dropout rate.

The second phase of the study focused on the potential impact of size on dropout rate. A model was studied, analyzing the direct influence of school size on the diversity of academic offerings and on school social climate, as well as the indirect effect on dropout rate. Strong links were found between size and the factors of program diversity and social climate.

Increasing the size of the school does, in fact, influence the variety of courses and programs available, as well as the general social climate. The larger the school, the greater the program diversity, but the less positive the social climate. (p. 341)

The study further found that school social climate has a stronger influence than program diversity on dropout rate.

Finally, the study investigated which of the components of school social climate and of program diversity contributed most to the influence on dropout rate. Correlation coefficients and regression analysis indicated that problems within the social environment and the level of participation—social climate factors—

had the highest relationship with dropout rate. Other studies also support the findings that student involvement in school activities and the severity of the general problems at the school have the greatest impact on the dropout rate.

Similar analysis of program diversity indicated that specific academic program and course availability are most related to the overall dropout rate. Though the coefficient between program diversity and dropout rate was quite low (.09 percent), diversity in academics seems more important than diversity in facilities.

What Are Possible Implications for School Improvement?

The most direct implications of this study are in the area of school consolidation. When small schools are consolidated into megaschools, the quality of school environment is sacrificed. Increasing the size of a high school may produce a rise in the dropout rate. Larger student bodies tend to produce a less positive social environment, less social integration, and less identity with the school. This may result in more students leaving school prematurely.

For big schools already experiencing large dropout rates, more attention to the social dimensions associated with dropouts may provide helpful clues for reducing the ratio of dropouts.

— Frank X. Ferris

EFFECTIVE SCHOOLS RESEARCH ABSTRACTS

SAFE AND ORDERLY ENVIRONMENT

CITATION: Berner, Maureen M., "Building Conditions, Parental Involvement, and Student Achievement in the District of Columbia Public School System," *Urban Education* 28, 1 (April 1993): 6-29.

What Did the Researcher Do?

Can parent involvement have an impact on the physical conditions of school buildings? Does the physical condition of school buildings affect the achievement of the students attending that school? These are the major questions addressed in this study of schools in the Washington, D.C. school district, where the researcher found the state of school buildings to be alarming. "Problems ranged from toilet stall doors missing in restrooms and numerous broken windows to nonfunctioning fire-alarm systems and entire buildings recommended for closing." (p. 6) Berner notes that the problem of deteriorating infrastructures in school buildings exists across the country, especially in urban areas. A review of recent studies documents the conclusion that the poor physical conditions in public schools affect not only the safety and operational efficiency of the school, but also can have an impact on student attitudes toward school. A building in poor repair contributes to the attitude and discipline problems among students, which, in turn, contributes to poor performance in schools. A deteriorating building tells students that the society does not place a value on education.

In 1987, when this study was initiated, the public school system in Washington, D.C. included 191 educational facilities serving about 83,000 students. The GPA of high school students was 1.73 on a 4-point scale. The poor physical conditions in many of the school buildings were documented in a 1989 report, issued by the Committee on Public Education (COPE), a 64-member group formed in 1988 to examine D.C. schools and develop a long-range plan to improve the educational system. COPE collected and analyzed school records and concluded that, during the three-year period 1986–1989, only 17 percent of the work orders requesting repair and maintenance were completed; the length of time between the work order and the response of the service personnel was three to six months. The researcher designed regression models to test two hypotheses:

- External factors are related to building conditions, and parents as primary constituents of schools can have a significant impact on the physical state of the school facility.

- Student academic achievement can be affected by the physical condition of the environment in the school.

Data for the analysis were collected from a number of sources. Parents United for the D.C. Public Schools, a parent advocacy group, enlisted the assistance of volunteers, including maintenance workers, engineers, and architects. COPE organized the volunteers into groups to visit each school and report on the building conditions and the adequacy of the facilities. The Urban League conducted a survey of 52 schools to document their level of parent involvement.

The first regression model tested the effect of parent involvement on conditions of school buildings. Parent involvement was measured by the PTA budget of the school and PTA membership, calculated on a per-student basis. The premise was that a PTA with more funds in its budget would have more influence over repairs, maintenance, and other building conditions. Several other variables included in the model were:

- school level—elementary or secondary

- age of the school building

- neighborhood characteristics—income level and percentage of white population

- school enrollment

The second model, designed to test whether the condition of the school building is statistically correlated with academic achievement, also included the variables listed above. The independent variable, student achievement, was measured by scores from the Comprehensive Tests of Basic Skills. The first model was run on the schools surveyed by the Urban League; complete data were available on only 41 of the 52 schools in the original sample. The second model was tested on both the sample schools and the data set including all of the D.C. schools.

What Did the Researcher Find?

Impact of parent involvement on building conditions. The regression analysis revealed three significant variables which affect the physical condition of the schools. The age of the building was expected to correlate with the building conditions, but was found to have much less significance than anticipated. Elementary schools tended to have better conditions than secondary schools. School enrollment was significant, with the larger schools more likely to have a fair or excellent physical plant. This analysis also confirmed the correlation between parent involvement and school conditions. The model relating parental involvement and building conditions explained 10 percent to 28 percent of the total variance. As the PTA budget per pupil increased, the improvement in building conditions demonstrated a significant rise.

Impact of building conditions on student achievement. The regression analysis of this model revealed that the two neighborhood variables (mean income and percentage of white population) have a significant correlation with student achievement. The school enrollment variable was found to have a negative relationship with student achievement. As school enrollment increased, the average student achievement score decreased. "This model shows that an increase of 100 students can reduce the average achievement scores by 8.8 points." (p. 23)

The major finding of the study confirms the hypothesis that building conditions can have a significant impact on student achievement. The model relating building condition and student achievement explained 23 percent to 34 percent of the total variance. "As a school moves from one category to the next, such as poor to fair, average achievement scores can be expected to increase by 5.455 points. If a school were to improve its conditions from poor to excellent, we could predict an increase of 10.9 points in the average achievement scores." (p. 23) The researcher

is careful to point out several limitations in the models. Data on parent involvement were available for only 41 schools—fewer than one-quarter of the schools in the district. Moreover, these schools did not represent a random sample, but probably tended to be schools with an active PTA, available to respond to the Urban League survey. This may have resulted in a bias in the analysis. The author points out that there may be unmeasured or unmeasurable variables in the second model which could affect student achievement, but were not included in the regression analysis.

What Are Possible Implications for School Improvement?

Although the research for this article was conducted in the District of Columbia, the results are applicable to other school systems, especially those in urban areas with older school buildings. Parent groups, which have formed to work on school improvement and reform, often place emphasis on such educational issues as curriculum and test scores and may feel that efforts related to maintenance, repair, and the physical conditions of school buildings are peripheral to the major educational problems.

This article emphasizes two significant conclusions: the physical condition of schools does have an impact on student achievement and parent involvement can affect building conditions. These important findings should convince parents to add this topic to their list of critical issues to address. This study should also encourage school administrators and school board members to recognize that safe and well-maintained schools kept in good repair are important influences on student attitudes and student achievement.

Noting that expenditures for building improvement are often the first victims of budget cuts, Berner urges policymakers to recognize that this problem not only affects future budgets, but also current students. She might well have concluded with Ron Edmonds' comment: "It matters whether or not you repair a broken window. It has less to do with the window and more to do with the fact that if it stays broken, you'll see it for a long time, and you'll conclude that nobody cares about the school."[1]

— Nancy Berla

[1] *A Conversation Between James Comer and Ronald Edmonds: Fundamentals of Effective School Improvement,* National Center for Effective Schools Research and Development, Kendall/Hunt Publishing Company, Dubuque, IA, 1989, p. 18.

EFFECTIVE SCHOOLS RESEARCH ABSTRACTS

SAFE AND ORDERLY ENVIRONMENT

CITATION: Oxley, Diana, "Organizing Schools Into Small Units: Alternatives to Homogeneous Grouping," *Phi Delta Kappan* 75, 7 (March 1994): 521-526.

What Did the Researcher Do?

Despite numerous studies and serious debate, the issue of homogeneous versus heterogeneous grouping of students for academic purposes is still a raging controversy among educational practitioners. As schools have increased in size, students have been steered into different academic tracks. But, this has resulted in lower-track students falling further behind, because the curriculum they receive lacks the challenge and academic rigor experienced by their more successful peer group. Educators have acted on the assumption that "students have different aptitudes for learning and, thus, require educational materials of varying difficulty." (p. 521) Recent advancements in the cognitive sciences have challenged these assumptions. At the same time, economic demands for workers with higher-level skills have intensified the need for increased academic competence by all graduates.

"Today, high schools in the United States often enroll as many as 3,000 students. Yet, schools this large are difficult to defend on educational grounds. Research indicates that large school size adversely affects attendance, school climate, and student involvement in school activities." (p. 521) Instead, the author proposes organizing schools into small subunits to serve all students better and especially to provide improved academic instruction for special needs and remedial students. "My purpose...[in this article] is to describe an approach to small-unit organization that provides alternatives to the practices of sorting students and grouping homogeneously," says Oxley. "Since this approach challenges deeply rooted educational methods, I also discuss some of the ways that educators have overcome professional and political obstacles to reform." (p. 522)

The designs for two schools, Koln-Holweide (a German comprehensive secondary school) and William Penn High School (a predominantly African-American campus in Philadelphia), are described in detail and presented as firsthand examples of successful implementation of the small-unit technique to meet "students' diverse academic needs in 'regular' classrooms. These schools incorporate structural features of small-unit design that have come to be associated with greater teacher knowledge of students, a sense of community among students, and higher rates of attendance and academic achievement." (p. 522)

What Did the Researcher Find?

Koln-Holweide serves approximately 1,600 students, with a lower school of Grades 5–10 and an upper school of Grades 11–13 for college-bound students. Twenty-five percent of the student body is composed of Turkish immigrants, and many students are from poor, single parent families; yet "almost all students complete 10th grade on time, compared to a national dropout rate of 14%." (p. 522) The school operates on a "horizontal small-unit plan in which all the students at a given grade level are grouped with the same teachers for six years" from Grades 5 through 10. (p. 523) Each grade level contains about 225 students, 18 to 22 teachers, and a grade-level leader, who also teaches part-time. "When students begin the fifth grade, disabled, Turkish, slow- and fast-learning, and male and female students are distributed equally among the three teams...Special education students, including those with behavioral problems and physical and intellectual disabilities, are mainstreamed at Koln-Holweide...Specialists work with students in the context of their regular classes...In core subject classes, students work almost entirely in table groups...[which] are heterogeneous in terms of gender, ethnicity, and ability. The students belong to the same table groups in each course throughout the year...[and] are expected to help one another and to contribute to the group's mastery of the work." (p. 523)

William Penn High School serves approximately 1,800 students in Grades 9–12, many of whom are poor and qualify for the free lunch program. A high number are eligible for Chapter 1 and special education programs. The school uses a "vertical small-unit plan [in which] each unit contains students from all grade levels." (p. 524) The units have a variety of curricular themes and provide instruction in both core and theme subjects. The author focuses on the operation of one unit, The House of Masterminds, because it was "designed to serve a student population in which one-half of ninth-graders had previously failed to be promoted. House staff members raised standards, adopted African-American culture as a curricular theme, and individualized instruction." (p. 524) This unit serves approximately 250 students at the 9–10 level, using a staff of 11 teachers—including a Chapter 1 reading specialist and special education instructor. Teams remain with the same groups of students for two years. Each team member teaches his or her subject to four classes of students, and also teaches one African-American studies class.

"Staff members do not organize students by ability. A remedial math class that many ninth-graders used to take was eliminated in the House and replaced with algebra. Similarly, Chapter 1-eligible students are not programmed separately for reading remediation classes. Instead, the Chapter 1 reading specialist collaborates with the interdisciplinary teams in developing strategies to improve students' reading skills in the context of core subject areas and directly assists students in the classroom. Special education students are mainstreamed within the House of Masterminds; a maximum of three such students are assigned to any one class…House staff members use adaptive instruction…[a] strategy [which] assumes that all students have unique strengths and weaknesses that respond better to individualized and group instruction than to exclusive reliance on whole-class instruction…students who have not mastered the material covered receive a grade of incomplete until they have completed it successfully…One full day [a week] is devoted to seminars…in which students are free to pursue a topic of their choice during the morning and either remedial or enrichment work in the afternoon." (p. 524)

Both the schools described by the researcher have successfully reorganized teaching and learning in ways that have proved successful for students who have difficulty in more traditional educational settings. The campuses have accomplished their tasks while continually dealing with resistance from prevailing practices and philosophies.

What Are Possible Implications for School Improvement?

The author offers solutions to two critical problems. The first is the proliferation of large high schools with specialized curriculum offerings to meet the perceived needs of students with varying abilities. The second problem is the unproductive practice of segregating students of different achievement levels and socioeconomic backgrounds into homogeneous tracks, in an attempt to match their abilities to different curricula offerings. Thus, schools function as agents that sort and select students into career paths according to the quality of educational opportunities they receive.

Research clearly indicates the ineffectiveness of large high schools in meeting the academic and social needs of students. The author proposes "dividing large schools into small units, or subschools…[in order to create] a context for teaching and learning that is more stable, more intimate, and more supportive…Organizing schools by units encourages a coordinated, cross-disciplinary approach to instruction [and the adults] take collective responsibility for their students' success…Small-unit organization also has the potential to bring about significant changes in the traditional shape of school governance…[because they] lend themselves to a decentralized system." (p. 522) The use of small-unit organization by the two schools depicted in the article clearly demonstrates the positive impact of such a heterogeneous arrangement. At William Penn, the staff "altered their methods of teaching instead of their expectations for those who [did] not adapt to traditional schools…students of varying backgrounds and educational histories [had] an equal chance to succeed." (p. 526) This was accomplished through the reorganization of existing academic tracks and special needs programs and the adoption of instructional methods that allowed teachers "to meet diverse student needs in a common context." (p. 526)

If educational leaders are willing to implement the strategies presented by this author, "separate but unequal" schooling might finally become an educational relic of America's past.

— Judy Wilson Stevens

Section III

Student

Discipline

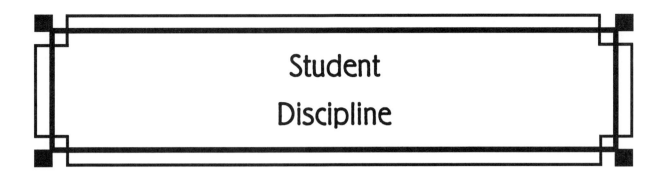

Student
Discipline

Looking at the organization of a school may provide valuable information about the causes of and solutions for disruptive student behavior.

- Schools that practice decentralized decision making have fewer student disciplinary problems.

- Student ownership and involvement in solving problems, along with an emphasis on teaching students leadership skills, create an atmosphere that promotes self-discipline.

- Principals who are strong leaders and willing to listen create a climate that discourages disruptive behavior.

- Schools with minimal disciplinary problems show administrative support for teachers who take leadership roles in handling student disputes.

- Discipline codes that are created with input from teachers, administrators, students, and parents are most likely to be successful.

- Fewer disciplinary problems occur in schools which offer a myriad of opportunities for students to feel successful at school tasks.

- An emphasis on prevention and positive behavior helps to reduce behavioral problems.

- An emphasis on academic excellence also helps to reduce behavioral problems.

- Consistent rules, evenly enforced throughout the school, create a more stable, positive environment.

- Clean, aesthetically pleasing surroundings give students evidence that others care about them; as a result, they care about their school behavior.

- Teachers and administrators who are willing to discuss a problem with a student at any time, and who demonstrate the presence of respect, intentionality, optimism, and trust are likely to deal with students who respond in kind.

In summary, high expectations for students' moral development are just as important as high expectations for their cognitive development.

EFFECTIVE SCHOOLS RESEARCH ABSTRACTS

SAFE AND ORDERLY ENVIRONMENT

CITATION: Short, Paula M. and Rick Jay Short, "Beyond Techniques: Personal and Organizational Influences on School Discipline," *High School Journal* (October/November 1987): 31-36.

What Did the Researchers Do?

In a review of the literature on school discipline, the researchers found that it concentrated heavily on descriptions of particular techniques and programs that assumed a strong link between student behavior and discipline techniques. The reviewers hypothesized that this approach may be simplistic. "Disruptive behaviors often have multiple causes, only some of which lie in the classroom." (p. 31)

They proposed that "techniques may often be less important than organization, awareness, and communication in striving to help classrooms be more safe and orderly." (p. 31)

The authors cited Wayson, who reports that numerous discipline problems can be related to the ways in which schools are organized and managed, and staff are trained.[1]

What are some of the evident characteristics of well-disciplined schools?

- Ongoing training and attention to cooperative problem solving.

- Decentralized decision-making authority.

- Student involvement in and ownership of problems.

- Rules and procedures that encourage responsibility.

- Individualized instruction.

- A school-wide awareness and respect for personal characteristics and problems which affect both student and staff behavior.

- Consistent school/home cooperation.

- An organizational arrangement and a physical plant that facilitates this type of contextual milieu.

What Did the Researchers Find?

The literature revealed several environmental variables related to the larger view of school discipline processes. "Not only are these variables important…but their interaction may also influence the nature of discipline in the school social system." (p. 32)

Administrator variables. Because administrators influence the setting of goals for the school, the tone they establish is crucial to maintaining a school climate conducive to teaching and learning. In a well-disciplined school, a principal would be perceived as supporting teachers who take the leadership role in handling discipline problems. "Neither principals nor teachers want school administrators to function primarily as enforcers." (p. 33)

Finally, the researchers describe the role and power of the principal. The role of the administrator, if supervisory, carries a positive, social influence that can help prevent or minimize discipline problems.

Teacher variables. Teachers bear most of the responsibility, not only for the use for any imposed discipline techniques, but for the overall smooth running of the class. A teacher's philosophy of discipline is a crucial consideration. Willower described a continuum.[2] At one extreme are educators whose philosophy is custodial, based on beliefs that children will learn in a well-ordered, highly structured setting, which offers little accommodation for children's individual differences. At the other extreme is the humanistic educator who believes that students are intrinsically motivated, naturally positive, and able, with appropriate guidance, to problem solve.

There is also wide variation in a teacher's own perception of what constitutes a discipline problem. Custodial educators will cite a list of problem behaviors and may have a bag of intervention techniques at hand. Humanistic educators believe that, given the right conditions, students want to and will improve their behaviors. "Thus, discipline philosophy may determine perception of discipline problems, as well as the acceptability of discipline techniques in the classroom." (p. 34)

Organizational variables. The researchers group these variables in three ways:

1. **Beliefs and strategies.** It appears that discipline strategies will be more widely carried out if they match closely with the beliefs of the educators who work in the school.

2. **Between administrators and teachers.** "Disagreements between administrators and faculty may cause conflict, covert resistance, and alienation." (p. 34) While a perfect match of philosophies is unlikely, awareness of the staff's positions, effective consistent communications, and compromises will be necessary for dealing with discipline problems effectively.

3. **Involvement and alienation.** Wayson pointed out that school conditions which negatively affect staff members are more important "causes" of disruptive behavior than any condition found within individual students.[3] He cautioned that depersonalization of faculty and students creates a setting in which discipline problems will flourish. A climate which encourages student participation in school activities, gives them status, visibility, and recognition, and an orientation to their school culture is most likely to reduce disruptive behavior.

What Are Possible Implications for School Improvement?

In an effective school, working to become even more effective, the interaction and strengthening of the seven effective schools correlates is an integral part of the local school's improvement effort. A key part of the improvement framework is collaborative problem solving. Discipline becomes more of an ongoing, focused dialogue and concern, which emphasizes not control, but shared responsibility.

Tightening controls, and seeing students as problems, can create a narrow and undesirable approach. Instead, personal and organizational characteristics should be examined and taken into account. The role of everyone in the school should be considered. Looking at the organization may provide valuable information about both the causes and solutions for student misbehavior.

— Beverly A. Bancroft

[1] W.W. Wayson, "The Politics of Violence in the Schools: Double Speak and Disruptions in Public Confidence," *Phi Delta Kappan* 67, 2 (1985): 127-132.

[2] D.J. Willower, "Some Comments on Inquiries on Schools and Pupil Control," *Teachers College Record* 77, 2 (1975): 221-230.

[3] Wayson, op. cit., p. 129.

SAFE AND ORDERLY ENVIRONMENT

CITATION: Lasley, Thomas J. and William W. Wayson, "Characteristics of Schools with Good Discipline," *Educational Leadership* (Fall 1982): 28-31.

What Did the Researchers Do?

In 1979, the Phi Delta Kappan (PDK) Commission on Discipline began to investigate the discipline phenomenon in schools by identifying exemplary schools, where discipline was not a significant problem. Commission members reviewed data on the demographics of each school and on the characteristics of each school's program.

They found that schools with effective discipline practices were characterized by certain distinguishing features. Lasley and Wayson have reviewed and analyzed the commission's study. Their discussion of the five characteristics that appeared most striking in schools with good discipline should provide other schools with the basis for understanding how discipline problems can be dealt with effectively.

What Did the Researchers Find?

Characteristic 1—All faculty members and students are involved in problem solving. These exemplary schools foster a positive environment through the inclusion of all members of the school community in solving problems—including discipline problems. Discipline is considered to be a matter that concerns everyone—not just the few who have broken rules. These exemplary schools generally developed discipline codes, which were usually drawn up with input from students, teachers, and administrators. At one school, all three groups, plus parents, were represented on a committee that drafted a new discipline code. Later, a full school day was given over to teaching the new code to students, with members of the committee working with groups of 25 students, answering questions and explaining rules and regulations.

In an environment of community involvement, administrators and teachers are more ready to search for solutions to problems before they become serious, rather than ferret out victims. For example, in one school, where graffiti had been a problem, the school initiated a number of mural-painting projects on the walls of the school halls. Coordinated by the art teacher, the student murals made the school's interior more attractive, and vandalism and graffiti decreased significantly.

Characteristic 2—The school is viewed as a place to experience success. Students need to feel successful at school tasks. Success contributes to self-esteem and, in turn, to more positive student behavior. Schools which provide students with opportunities to experience success, through practicing skills and developing concepts, tend to have fewer discipline problems. Teachers must be willing to give respect to students, as well as receive it from them.

An emphasis on training students in leadership skills helps to create an atmosphere which promotes the development of individual self-discipline, in which students work together to achieve common goals.

Characteristic 3—Problem solving focuses on causes rather than symptoms. It is important for teachers and administrators to develop an understanding of the underlying causes of discipline problems, rather than focusing exclusively on punishment for those who break the rules. Many discipline problems are symptomatic of other problems in the school environment which are not being dealt with. One school found it helpful to make three lists related to discipline problems—one of symptoms, one of causes, and one of activities that might ameliorate the causes. The symptoms list included such familiar problems as vandalism, disrespect for people, student disinterest, and failing test scores. The causes included lack of student involvement, lack of rules on attendance and discipline, wishy-washy leadership, staff concerned with self-preservation, and parent apathy. And the activities suggested for dealing with these problems included written rules and consistent enforcement, staff cooperation, support of staff by administration, communication and meetings with parents, and a student handbook.

By treating causes, rather than symptoms, the school placed ownership of the problems on the full school community.

Characteristic 4—The emphasis is on positive behavior and preventive measures. These exemplary schools are aware of the limitations of punishment, seeing it as a last resort. The commission cited findings by Rohrkemper and Brophy that those teachers with the greatest ability to handle difficult students were those who were more supportive, used more rewards (including symbolic rewards), and gave more comfort and reassurance to their students.[1] Less effective teachers were far less supportive—and used punishment more often.

The exemplary schools gave much attention to positive reinforcement of student behavior, with activities to enhance self-perceptions (such as honor days), positive messages to parents, and special programs to recognize student accomplishments. Such activities support the more subtle reinforcement that teachers gave in the classroom.

Characteristic 5—The principal is a strong leader. The Commission's study, like many others, stressed the importance of strong leadership in an effective school. "Similarly, the principal plays a prominent role with regard to discipline, and no person has as great an impact on the school atmosphere." (p. 31) The principal supplies the teachers with the support and leadership they need in maintaining an orderly classroom. At the same time, the effective principal respects the teachers' instructional autonomy. Putting this ideal into practice requires a principal who is willing to listen. The researchers cited the case of a principal who began work in a new school by talking individually to everyone on the staff and asking them about needed changes in the school. His leadership began subtly, and he was careful, but willing, to delegate responsibility. His willingness to listen was mentioned by teachers as a major factor in his successful leadership.

What Are Possible Implications for School Improvement?

The five characteristics discussed here are only some of the findings reported by the PDK Commission. A more complete discussion is available in the publication, *Handbook for Developing Schools with Good Discipline*, which presents many other factors helpful to schools in understanding and dealing with their discipline problems.[2]

Perhaps the most significant finding emerging from this study is that there is no single recipe for success. Those who have been looking for simple solutions to the discipline problem will probably not find them in the PDK Commission study. On the other hand, those who are willing to reexamine their current practices and try new approaches may discover the findings to be a useful guide to action.

— Kate O'Neill

---

[1] Rohrkemper, M., and J. Brophy, *Teachers' General Strategies for Dealing with Problem Students.* Institute for Effective Research on Teaching, East Lansing, MI, 1980, p. 14.

[2] Wayson, W.W., et al., *Handbook for Developing Schools with Good Discipline.* Phi Delta Kappa, Bloomington, IN, 1982.

EFFECTIVE SCHOOLS RESEARCH ABSTRACTS

SAFE AND ORDERLY ENVIRONMENT

CITATION: Gaddy, Gary D., "High School Order and Academic Achievement," *American Journal of Education* (August 1988): 496-518.

What Did the Researcher Do?

It is commonly assumed and widely stated that there is a direct relationship between the discipline of a school and the achievement of its students. But supporting research data that would raise this contention above the level of a common presumption are sparse. Most of the literature cited stems from the effective schools research, which concentrates primarily upon elementary schools. Secondary schools, by their very nature, deal with student behavior issues which are substantially different from those encountered in elementary schools.

To begin the process of elevating common opinion to knowledge based upon research, the researcher reviewed several key quantitative studies which examined school order and achievement at the secondary level.

Two major studies provide useful information on the relationship between school order and achievement. They are Fifteen Thousand Hours[1] and the High School and Beyond Project.[2]

Fifteen Thousand Hours was a longitudinal study of 12 inner-city London high schools. After controlling for differences in various "intake" measures, such as prior achievement, behavior, and student background, the researchers were able to develop conclusions about the impact of school effects upon students.

The High School and Beyond Project was a massive study of representative students from over 1,000 high schools, public and private, selected as representative of all American high schools. The basic methodology was a number of survey instruments designed to address a multitude of questions about educational practice and policy.

Because of its large scale, the project provides a base to study school-level processes.

What Did the Researcher Find?

The Fifteen Thousand Hours project, conducted by Rutter and his colleagues, found that differences between high schools do make a difference for students. Schools that emphasize academics had better student behavioral outcomes. In particular, frequency of homework for first-year students was associated with good behavior, even more than it was associated with achievement. This may be because the homework symbolized the school's academic emphasis and its expectation that its pupils had the ability and self-discipline needed to succeed.

This confirms the finding of the Safe School Study which found that the "troubled schools" that turned around seemed to be the ones that had begun to emphasize the importance of academic excellence.[3]

Rutter noted certain other characteristics in those high schools which had less misbehavior and less delinquency:

- Behavior expectations and discipline standards are consistent across the school, rather than left to individual teachers.

- At both the school and classroom level, rewards and praise for good schoolwork and for behavior are strongly related to good behavior.

- Fewer behavioral problems occur in schools where teachers are willing to discuss a problem with a student at any time.

- The cleaner, more aesthetically pleasing a school, the fewer behavioral problems.

The latter two findings suggest that, the more students see evidence that others care about them and their school, the more care they take regarding their school behavior.

In summary, the researchers of Fifteen Thousand Hours conclude that school processes constituted the predominant influence on children's behavior in the classroom and the playground. Further, the correlation between achievement and behavior suggests that schools with good discipline have good achievement, and vice versa.

The High School and Beyond Project did not specifically address the relationship between behavior and achievement, as did the Fifteen Thousand Hours project. Therefore, the findings which can be drawn on this topic from the project are not as firm as those drawn from the Fifteen Thousand Hours study. The High School and Beyond Project provides "weak" evidence that perceived differences in student orderliness might be partly responsible for student achievement.

What Are Possible Implications for School Improvement?

What is the basic purpose of education? Is it to have students who are well behaved, who do not disrupt the school?

Planning teams which are seeking either to resolve a serious school-wide discipline problem or merely to improve discipline could easily install a set of rules and regulations which would cause behavior to improve, but were excessive. "Optimal environmental order (in a school) may (or should) fall short of that found in a Marine Corps boot camp or a well-run prison." (p. 513) But if a school installs rules and regulations as ends in themselves, "it may be fostering a superficial order that is detrimental to self-discipline." (p. 513)

On the other hand, if the basic purpose of public education is to learn, then the research cited from the Fifteen Thousand Hours project and the Safe School Study offers a significant roadmap to building planning teams seeking to improve discipline: schools should emphasize academics to improve student behavioral outcomes.

Further, the researcher offers a number of specific findings that schools should consider as they decide how to improve the quantity and quality of learning.

A school environment which fosters an ordered discipline of the mind and the ultimate goal of self-discipline occurs only when both students and staff choose to obey the code of conduct. This behavior comes from consent. Where behavior "comes only by force, external order may be achieved, but the ultimate purpose of education may be thwarted. Schools that impose order, rather than cultivating it, may win no more than an uneasy truce while, at the same time, losing the hearts and minds of their students." (p. 514)

One clear suggestion of Fifteen Thousand Hours is that "schools that focus their attention on order (apparently as an end) not only fail to accomplish their intermediate goal, but their greater mission of academics as well." (pp. 514-515)

Building planning teams who are working to install the correlate of safe and orderly environment would be well advised to consider the researcher's conclusions carefully.

— Robert E. Sudlow

[1] Rutter, M., B. Maughan, P. Mortimore, J. Ouston, and A. Smith, *Fifteen Thousand Hours: Secondary Schools and Their Effects on Children*. Harvard University Press, Cambridge, MA, 1979.

[2] Coleman, J.S., T. Hoffer, and S. Kilgore, *High School Achievement: Public, Catholic and Other Private Schools Compared*. Basic Books, New York, NY, 1982.

[3] National Institute of Education, *Violent Schools—Safe Schools: Safe School Study*. Vol. 1., Government Printing Office, Washington, D.C. 1978.

CITATION: Reed, Charlotte and David B. Strahan, "Gentle Discipline in Violent Times," *Journal for a Just and Caring Education* 1 (July 1995): 320-333.

What Did the Researchers Do?

School safety often ranks at the top of the list of concerns when educators, parents, or politicians are asked to prioritize the most critical issues related to school improvement. Increasing numbers of assaults and murders plaguing our nation's campuses have led to a common "get-tough" response from school officials and their constituents. Some states, such as Texas, have created a "zero tolerance" stance toward disruptive students. Even so, reports of violence in schools have continued to rise despite these policies.

The authors "believe that a get-tough stance reflects a misperception of the problem of violence in schools." (p. 321) They believe that "issues of violence in schools are closely intertwined with issues of poverty and power." (p. 321) Citing examples of how professional negotiators handle threatening situations, the authors suggest that a gentle response to student violence may be more successful than current measures.

What Did the Researchers Find?

Three connected questions are explored as the researchers seek to present a different map for considering the problem of school violence: "(a) Why do students sometimes choose violence? (b) Why do we often choose a get-tough stance? and (c) How can we develop a gentle stance toward violent students and tough situations?" (p. 322)

To answer the question of why students sometimes choose violence, the authors describe the "layers of violence" in which today's students reside. (p. 322) Noting that "violence comprises the majority of the news and pervades every form of entertainment media," the authors concur with Marian Wright Edelman when she asserts that "our children are growing up today in an ethically polluted nation." (p. 322) Violence is glorified as heroes and villains

use it to get what they want. Some students live in very violent neighborhoods and witness drive-by shootings, drug deals, and families held hostage by roving gangs. "Many choose violence to deal with the anger and frustration." (pp. 322-323)

Students resort to violence in schools in an effort to protect themselves, because they do not feel "the adults, teachers, counselors, administrators, or security guards" can do so. (p. 323) Random acts of violence sometimes result in a retaliatory mentality by teachers against students. As a consequence, trivial incidents may be escalated into major confrontations when adults use extreme measures to respond to minor student offenses.

Students sometimes choose violence because "the cultural context of school situations may implicitly encourage aggression." (p. 324) Students may pick on or put down other students because of the existence of "a cultural context that values success that is defined in a hierarchical fashion." (p. 324) The authors "conclude that students sometimes choose violence because they need to establish a sense of control over troubling events they encounter." (p. 324)

If teachers can develop a better understanding about why students sometimes choose violence, they may be better able to examine the schools' response to violent behavior. To respond to the question of why we often choose a get-tough stance, the authors suggest that "our responses are shaped by two inter-acting value systems: our personal views of teaching and the collective cultures of our schools." (p. 325)

Teachers who view themselves as "confident and competent" are more likely to perceive students as "valuable, able, and responsible." (p. 326) When teachers hold this view of students and themselves, they are more likely to create a climate of trust, and focus on developing self-discipline in students.

Teachers who "view disruptions as threatening" are "more likely to respond in a defensive fashion." (p. 326) Their responses frequently include an aggressive physical stance, raised voice, and a shift from instruction to control, all of which "project a confrontational stance." (p. 326) In situations where students already feel threatened, perceived confrontational behavior by the teacher often "escalates tensions." (p. 326)

Teachers who work with at-risk students may intensify the level of confrontation in the classroom by the attitudes they possess about their work. Teachers with a success orientation are "more likely to believe all students can learn, demonstrate higher expectations, and accept more responsibility for creating connections." (p. 326) Their counterparts, who possess "the school of hard knocks orientation," expect less of their students, and are "more likely to refer them to special programs and often blame students' lack of success on cultural factors." (p. 326) They are also more likely to adopt a "get-tough stance toward the possibility of violence." (p. 326)

School cultures with a control orientation often emphasize power as the dominant structure for planning and discipline. "Maintaining control becomes the primary agenda of schooling." (p. 327)

The authors conclude that the view of control "seems basic to the ways we view ourselves and our students and, consequently, to the ways we respond to the possibilities of violence. A get-tough stance reflects a value orientation toward teacher control. We advocate a posture of shared control and believe that a gentle stance is more likely to invite a sense of empowerment." (p. 327)

In order to develop a gentle stance toward violent students and tough situations, the authors recommend the four essential components of Invitational Education: respect, intentionality, optimism, and trust. Not only are these characteristics needed in the classroom, but they must permeate the overall school.

Respect is the first requirement for creating a gentle stance toward violence. Many students have learned to "act tough to protect themselves." (p. 327) Respect may begin by acknowledging that "acting tough may have become part of their identity." (p. 327) These students are at a disadvantage when "we take away their survival tactics without giving them strategies that work both in school and out." (p. 328) Respect is not something students must earn; it is "an undeniable birthright of each human being." (p. 328)

Intentionality requires schools to deliberately plan to "empower students to make responsible choices to encourage shared control." (p. 329) Before school begins, plans must be "developed to teach students proactive strategies for coping with potentially violent situations." (p. 329) Teachers are encouraged to use a gentle tone of voice, nonthreatening language, and to avoid sarcasm. Excessively long lists of rules governing student behavior should be replaced with a collaboratively developed student code of conduct that "defines the operating principles of the entire school community." (p. 330)

Optimism is essential because it allows educators to "see their students not as they are, but as they could be." (p. 330) Teachers who are successful with at-risk students believe that all of them can learn and have high expectations for their success. These teachers also believe that they are personally capable of making a difference for their students.

Trust is developed when respect, intentionality, and optimism are practiced in schools. If trust is created, teachers and students can work together to decrease violence. Trust is enhanced when students are "offered significant choices about what and how they learn," as well as "guidelines for evaluating, monitoring, and controlling their own behavior." (p. 331)

What Are Possible Implications for School Improvement?

Parents, politicians, and educators have consistently demanded tougher discipline policies as the solution to school violence. State legislatures and school boards have responded with tougher penalties; yet, school violence continues to increase. It would appear that another approach might be worth trying.

These authors offer a different mental model for responding to student violence which relies heavily on the effective school correlates of a safe and orderly environment and high expectations for success. Instead of escalating the problem by creating a school culture that is authoritarian and controlling, a warm, gentle environment is suggested. Educators are urged to share control and develop self-discipline in students. The result would be safer schools, more nurturing communities, and, ultimately, a better world.

— Judy Wilson Stevens

EFFECTIVE SCHOOLS RESEARCH ABSTRACTS

SAFE AND ORDERLY ENVIRONMENT

CITATION: Kohn, Alfie, *Beyond Discipline: From Compliance to Community.* Association for Supervision and Curriculum Development, Alexandria, VA, 1996.

What Did the Researcher Do?

Alfie Kohn, the author of several books on education and human behavior, wrote this book after observing teachers at work in classrooms who were reputed to be exceptional in some way. He was particularly interested in knowing how they handle discipline problems, hoping to get a better understanding of how outstanding teachers respond to misbehavior. However, he "rarely got the chance to see these teachers work their magic with misbehaving children because it seemed as though the children in their classes almost never misbehaved." (p. xi)

What made their classrooms so free of problem behaviors? It turns out to be what these teachers are doing, but also what they are not doing. "They are not concentrating on being effective disciplinarians. This is partly because they have better things to do, and those better things are preventing problems from developing in the first place. But it is also because discipline—at least as that word is typically used— actively interferes with what they are trying to accomplish." (p. xii)

He asserts that present methods of discipline or "classroom management," including recently developed models, are largely based on securing student compliance to adults' demands. (p. xii) These approaches are usually teacher-directed, and "typically driven by a remarkably negative set of beliefs about the nature of children." (pp. xii-xiii) Some of the models urge teachers to "lay down the law with children and coerce them into compliance." (p. xiii) Others are "wrapped in rhetoric about motivation and responsibility, dignity, and cooperation and self-esteem. Look carefully at the prescriptions in the books and videos that describe these programs, and you will find a striking resemblance to standard

old-time discipline." (p. xiii) Further, he concludes, these approaches often do not work.

Kohn offers "an alternative vision—one brought to life in those extraordinary classrooms I've visited. This alternative is neither a recipe nor a different technique for getting mindless compliance. It requires that we transform the classroom, give up some power, and reconsider the way we define and think about misbehavior." (p. xv)

What Did the Researcher Find?

It is vital to first examine one's assumptions, or theories, about the nature of children, since these theories are significant in determining how one will react to a child. It is particularly important to examine negatively held beliefs or assumptions about children's nature. How an adult acts towards a child, based on those beliefs, will usually have a significant impact on how the child will respond. "Label a particular child a troublemaker and watch him become one. View children in general as self-centered, and that is exactly the way they will come to act. Treat students 'as if they need to be controlled' and you 'may well undermine their natural predispositions to develop self-controls and internalized commitments to upholding cultural norms and values.'" (p. 7)

More positive views of children have results that are just as powerful, often referred to as the "Pygmalion effect." (p. 7) Teachers can create a positive self-fulfilling prophecy when it comes to children's behavior. If a "teacher trusts her students to make decisions, they will act very differently from those in her colleague's classroom if left on their own; typically, they will act responsibly and go right on with their learning." (p. 8)

Most approaches to discipline focus on how to get students to do what adults want. Kohn believes that these approaches use various combinations of three basic themes: 1) coercion (just forcing the child to do something); 2) punishment (providing a negative consequence in order to change the student's future behavior); and 3) rewards (providing a positive consequence for complying with the adult). All of these approaches can work in the short run, but have fundamental problems which make them an inappropriate choice for the long run. The more we try to get student compliance through any of these means, "the more difficult it is for them to become morally sophisticated people who think for themselves and care about others." (p. 62)

Just as educators have come to understand that children should construct meaning as part of an optimal cognitive learning experience, ethical development also requires that the students "construct moral meaning" for themselves. (p. 67) Educators first need to abandon the "tools of traditional discipline," such as rewards and punishments. (p. 67) Beyond that, they need to overcome their "preoccupation with getting compliance" and instead have students involved in "the process of devising and justifying ethical principles." (p. 67)

To begin the process, teachers need to think about their long-term goals for their students, and identify assumptions and practices which are in conflict with the need to move beyond mere compliance in developing students' ethical practices. A constructivist approach to moral development challenges conventional approaches to classroom management and moves "beyond a focus on behavior, on rules, and on ending conflict." (p. 68) Constructivist thinking emphasizes the importance of developing maximum opportunities for students to make their own choices, as well as the creation of a caring classroom community, so students can make those choices together. To deal with issues which affect most of the class, Kohn recommends classroom meetings, which he says are the place for sharing, deciding, planning, and reflecting on issues of relevance.

In one eye-opening example, an elementary school teacher describes her difficulty in getting her class in on time after recess: "I told them how tired I was of

yelling at them to line up and how afraid I was that the principal was going to give me a poor rating because of all the time we wasted. Then I listened to them. I couldn't believe my ears. They said they were sick of standing out there in the hot sun waiting for me and asked why they had to line up anyway." (p. 79) After more discussion, a solution—suggested by one of the children—was agreed upon. When the "bell rang, they were to walk to the room from the playground. I was to walk from the teacher's lounge, and we'd go in." (p. 80) The compromise worked beautifully, and opened the door to student involvement in problem solving.

Kohn offers several suggestions on what might be done when problems do arise in the class. These include developing a trusting relationship with students, taking the time and effort to diagnose why a problem may have occurred, and encouraging maximum student involvement in the problem's solution and appropriate restitution. Students should be "encouraged to explore possibilities, reflect on their own motives, disagree, and, in general, to construct an authentic solution. This asks a lot of student and teacher alike—perhaps too much on some occasions. But anything short of this is not real problem solving and is not likely to produce worthwhile results." (p. 126)

What Are Possible Implications for School Improvement?

Affective development requires us to actively reflect on what students need to flourish and then work to provide that. We must first determine what the goal of affective development is and then must critically examine whether current practices are consistent with reaching that goal. The goal or purpose which is chosen depends on one's beliefs and assumptions about children.

Kohn is recommending a set of beliefs based upon high expectations for students' ability to develop ethical principles through their own active involvement in the process, not through coercion. High expectations for students' moral development need to be just as important in effective schools as high expectations for cognitive development.

— Lynn Benore

EFFECTIVE SCHOOLS RESEARCH ABSTRACTS

SAFE AND ORDERLY ENVIRONMENT

CITATION: Sylwester, Robert, "The Neurobiology of Self-Esteem and Aggression," *Educational Leadership* 54, 5 (February 1997): 75-79.

What Did the Researcher Do?

"Violent acts like gang-related murders, playground shootings, riots, suicides, and assaults in school are prominently featured in the news, but they aren't the norm in social interactions." (p. 75) This author contends that "7 percent of the population commits 80 percent of all the violent acts." (p. 75) He believes "violence is a limited social pathology" which begins with an impulsive act often triggered by "the aggressor's low level of self-esteem." (p. 75) The latest findings in the neurosciences, combined with a deeper understanding of the nature of self-esteem, may help shed light on what drives an individual into a violent act. More importantly, Sylwester says this knowledge can help schools reduce or eliminate violent behavior.

Recent discoveries from neurobiological research have revealed a connection between violent behavior and the level of the neurotransmitter, serotonin, a person possesses. Neurotransmitters are chemical substances in the brain that allow nerve cells to communicate. Serotonin is a "neurotransmitter that enhances relaxation and smooth/controlled motor coordination (by inhibiting quick motor responses). It regulates intestinal peristalsis, cardiovascular function, endocrine secretion, mood, pain, sexual activity, appetite, and behavior." (p. 77)

When an individual's life opportunities match the sense of self, serotonin levels remain adequate and self-esteem is healthy. On the other hand, if someone believes that they deserve a much better opportunity than life's circumstances are offering, self-esteem plummets and levels of serotonin drop. "Failure and negative social feedback inhibit the effects of serotonin and lead to lower self-esteem and possible violence." (p. 77)

What Did the Researcher Find?

"When young people see no hope to rise within mainstream society, they may create their own hierarchical gang cultures that provide them with opportunities to succeed within their counterculture's mores." (p. 77) People in both mainstream cultures and countercultures need a positive self-concept and self-esteem. According to this researcher, "successful people in mainstream society who decry gang symbols and exclusionary turf areas should look to the high-status symbols they use to flaunt their success and to their exclusionary golf courses and walled communities." (p. 77)

Research on stress has found that, in a stable societal hierarchy, "those at the bottom (who had little control over events) experienced far more stress and stress-related illness than those at the top." (p. 77) When the social hierarchy is unstable, "those currently at the top (whose power position was threatened) experienced the most stress and stress-related illness." (p. 77)

Implications for these findings suggest that "it is in the interest of the power elite (in community and classroom) to maintain social stability, and it is in the interest of the currently disenfranchised to create as much social instability (and classroom disruption) as possible in a desperate search for respect and success." (p. 77) If young people have few opportunities to succeed in the mainstream, we can expect more social instability. "It is in our best interest to support inclusionary policies that promote social goals and to enhance the powerful role that schools can play in helping students to seek their dreams." (p. 77)

Other findings "suggest that social feedback creates fluctuations from our basal serotonin levels, and these fluctuations help determine our current level of self-esteem." (p. 78) These vacillations in serotonin levels significantly affect whether we go through life "with the calm assurance that leads to smoothly controlled movements" or react to life's events with "irritability that leads to impulsive, uncontrolled, reckless, aggressive, violent, or suicidal behavior." (p. 77)

A high or low level of serotonin "isn't innate and permanent." (p. 78) Recent medical findings have allowed patients to use drugs and nutrition to help regulate their serotonin levels. Antidepressant drugs such as Prozac, Zoloft, and Paxil do not actually increase the amount of serotonin in the brain, but do allow the serotonin to remain active in the brain for a longer period of time. "These drugs block the reuptake channels on the terminal, and so slow down the reabsorption process." (p. 77) Generating an elevation in the effects of serotonin "often enhances a person's self-esteem; this increased optimism and happier mood lead to the positive social feedback that allows the natural system to take over again in time and to function effectively. Think of jump-starting a dead car battery—a few miles of driving will reenergize the battery, and it can then function on its own." (p. 79)

Nutrition researchers may have found a way to increase serotonin levels with diet changes that include increasing the consumption of carbohydrates. There appears to be "a connection between serotonin/ carbohydrate levels and emotionally driven eating disorders that emerge out of" stressful situations. (p. 79) Carbohydrates in our diet "enhance the entry of tryptophan into the brain, where it is converted into serotonin." (p. 77)

What Are Possible Implications for School Improvement?

Until recently, educators have put the responsibility for misbehavior squarely on the students' shoulders, adopting the attitude that students deliberately create disruption because they are inherently bad. The emerging research reported by this author may lead us to look for a biochemical imbalance as a possible contributor to violent behavior. Serotonin deficiency may play a significant role in impulsive acts which lead to aggression.

Although drugs and nutrition have been found to stabilize serotonin levels, the author asserts that the "best support for a serotonin deficiency is probably the natural system of positive social feedback that we have evolved over millennia." (p. 79) Positive feedback in the classroom is a "powerful social device for helping us to assess and define ourselves (self-concept) and to value ourselves (self-esteem)." (p. 79)

Schools can look inward to determine whether an inclusive environment allows all students the opportunity to achieve success. Portfolio assessment, journals, and creative artwork can encourage self-examination and enhance self-concept and self-esteem. Providing opportunities for students to work in groups where all contributions are valued can also increase perceptions of self-worth. Using cooperative learning strategies for conflict resolution could help students find out how to reduce negative behaviors.

All of these suggestions by the author can have a positive effect on school improvement. Instead of blaming students and society for the escalating violence in our schools, educators can look within the confines of the school climate to discover if changes could be made in operational procedures to allow all students an opportunity to participate in the mainstream culture. To the degree that this option is broadened, there will be less need for the creation of countercultures and gang behavior. The result will be a better educated populace and genuine preparation for each student to become a contributing member of society.

— Judy Wilson Stevens

Section IV

Classroom

Management

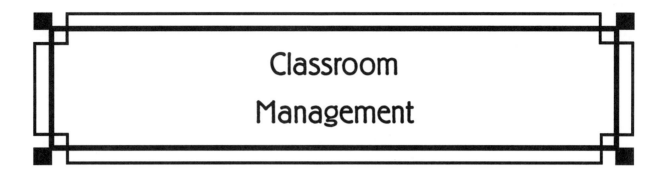

Classroom Management

Maintaining student engagement in school tasks through optimal classroom management is not only essential for obtaining the desired outcomes in learning, but also for steering students away from negative actions.

Effective classroom managers:

- Spend time before the school year begins to give careful consideration to the physical space of the classroom and how to best use it.

- Firmly establish rules and procedures at the beginning of the year, teach them with clarity, and enforce them consistently and systematically.

- Respond to misbehavior promptly.

- Emphasize accountability and accuracy in daily assignments.

- Monitor student work regularly.

- Organize their time, making sure materials are ready, and designing activities that are relevant and involve the student in his or her own learning.

- Give students many opportunities for cooperative group learning.

- Practice two skills—the ability to know what's going on in their classroom and the ability to attend to separate issues simultaneously.

- Understand and teach control theory based on the premise that all human behavior is generated by what goes on inside each person. They believe students should be taught that they have needs, are always trying to satisfy those needs, and the ways they behave are choices they make in the attempt to satisfy those needs.

- Recognize that orderly does not mean rigid and oppressive. It is possible to have a climate that encourages students to enjoy school.

- Celebrate successes and accomplishments.

While prevention is the goal in order to avoid disruptions, when they do occur, effective classroom managers handle them quickly and fairly.

EFFECTIVE SCHOOLS RESEARCH ABSTRACTS

SAFE AND ORDERLY ENVIRONMENT

CITATION: Evertson, Carolyn and Edmund T. Emmer, "Effective Management at the Beginning of the School Year in Junior High Classes," *Journal of Educational Psychology* 74, 4 (1982): 485-498.

What Did the Researchers Do?

Evertson and Emmers collected data in mathematics and English classes during the first three weeks of the school year. They studied the teaching behaviors of two groups of junior high school teachers who had been identified as being either more or somewhat less effective in their classroom management practices and outcomes. They hoped to isolate and describe behaviors which appeared, in a common-sense way, to promote more successful and focused outcomes for students.

Why did the researchers choose to study classroom management practice during the first three weeks of school? Maintaining student engagement in school tasks through optimal classroom management is essential to obtain the desired outcomes in the teaching/learning process. The researchers cited Jackson: "Certainly no educational goals are more immediate than those that concern the establishment and maintenance of the students' absorption in the task at hand."[1]

Why did they study both less and more effective classroom management styles? To enrich and verify their own and others' previous research, they built the "opening of school" study on existing teachers' classroom management practices in the context of both math and English. What behaviors, they asked, dependably occurred to set the stage for yearlong effective management practices to be assimilated into the school day? By observing these two sets of 13 classroom teachers and collecting and analyzing data, they were able to describe with accuracy these "antecedent" behaviors—practices, in place, that set the tone for the first and subsequent classroom teaching/learning situations.

What Did the Researchers Find?

More effective classroom managers were observed:

- to maintain higher on-task rates from students, especially at the beginning of the school year.

- to firmly establish rules and procedures for the year, to teach them with clarity, and well.

- to clearly specify expectations for students, and to assure understanding, so that "exceptions" discourse was neither distracting nor disruptive.

- to enforce their rules more consistently and systematically.

- to deal with disruptive behavior by reminding students of rules and then requiring compliance matter-of-factly.

- to be visibly vigilant about keeping students on task and be serious about active intervention.

- to be diligent in checking on how students completed assignments and used their in-class time.

- to use consistent grading practices for all types of assigned work, with emphasis on accountability and accuracy in daily assignments.

- to provide relevant activities.

- to be consistent in communicating assignments, objectives, goals, and expectations to students.

Compared to less effective classroom managers, the more effective managers were well-organized for their day and spent more time on the teaching task. They had materials ready; they were strong in designing involvement-type activities. The effective classroom managers who taught either English or math were rated higher than less effective managers in challenging the more able students.

What Are Possible Implications for School Improvement?

Both preservice and inservice professional education activities need to encompass training and reinforcement for the monitoring and enhancement of effective classroom management systems.

Not only teachers, but school administrators, need to review their antecedent behaviors in:

• planning classroom management;

• decision making about the styles and actions to be adopted; and

• envisioning the instructional year before it begins.

In the junior high setting, the researchers point out, students have attained more experience with going-to-school skills, so the junior high teacher's task is one essentially of communicating expectations clearly, monitoring subsequent behavior for compliance, and providing corrective feedback. Earlier, researchers found that teachers in elementary schools naturally gave more attention to rules and procedures, as students have their initial encounters with going to schools there.

To build and maintain a successful and high rate of student engagement on teaching and learning, practitioners are thus encouraged to make many crucial decisions and plans about the instructional year prior to the first day of school. School and classroom management practices can then focus visibly upon student/faculty engagement on teaching and learning during those first three weeks.

The authors conclude that the beginning of the year is clearly a critical time for establishing behavior patterns, expectations, and procedures that can persist throughout the year.

— Beverly A. Bancroft

---

[1] Jackson, P., *Life in Classrooms*. Holt, Rinehart, New York, NY, 1968.

EFFECTIVE SCHOOLS RESEARCH ABSTRACTS

SAFE AND ORDERLY ENVIRONMENT

CITATION: Copeland, Willis D., "Classroom Management and Student Teachers' Cognitive Abilities: A Relationship," *American Educational Research Journal* 24, 2 (Summer 1987): 219-236.

What Did the Researcher Do?

The recent research on classroom management has suggested that its importance derives from certain characteristics peculiar to the classroom. The classroom is seen as a multidimensional setting, in which many different events may occur over time. Many purposes are served; many different people are involved; and most of these "things" occur at the same time. As a result, teachers are required to possess a special set of managerial skills.

Two such skills have emerged from the early work of Kounin (1970). They are "withitness," or the teacher's ability to know what children are doing in the classroom—"teachers having eyes in the back of their heads,"—and, further, "overlap," or the ability to attend to separate issues simultaneously (attending to two or more things at the same time).

Cognitive psychologists have shown a research interest in the cognitive process of vigilance and multiple (split) attention. The purpose of this study was to determine whether a relationship exists between the two information-processing skills identified by the cognitive psychologists and the teacher behaviors identified by the classroom researchers.

The researcher sought to explore this possible relationship by the following research method. First, a microcomputer test battery, known as the "Classroom Drill Game," was created. In this test battery, each subject is presented with five separate tasks. The tasks require monitoring on-task activity of one pupil, assessing the responses of five other pupils, while presenting arithmetic problems to still other students. As a result of these simulations, five different performance measures are recorded.

Sixty-four elementary student teachers volunteered to be part of the study. All of them were nearing the conclusion of their practice teaching. The student teachers were observed during an actual classroom teaching situation, as well as the "Classroom Drill Game," and were measured as to the degree of their "withitness" and "overlap."

What Did the Researcher Find?

Several important findings emerged. First, clearly, the student teachers displayed a large variance in their abilities to score well on all measures taken. Second, a correlation of -.40 was found between a teacher's ability to practice these desirable classroom behaviors and the amount of time that students spend off-task. Third, the competency in the two cognitive skills as measured by the game was found to be a related factor in determining a teacher's success in creating classrooms that are characterized by high on-task behavior.

What Are Possible Implications for School Improvement?

The researcher's use of student teachers and his attempt to couple specific classroom behaviors of teachers with more general information-processing skills suggest several applications. To the extent that more generalized information-processing skills are tied to the subsequent presence or absence of desirable teacher behaviors, a test for these skills can be used either as a screening device to discourage those students who lack the needed skills from pursuing teaching—or it can be used as a diagnostic tool through which certain preservice training can be suggested and skills can be developed.

— Lawrence W. Lezotte

SAFE AND ORDERLY ENVIRONMENT

CITATION: Glasser, William M.D., *Control Theory in the Classroom.* Harper & Row, New York, NY, 1986.

What Did the Researcher Do?

In this book, William Glasser suggests specific means by which secondary schools can deal more effectively with unmotivated students. Dr. Glasser explains that nothing in the schools will change for the better until educators and others understand the error inherent in the stimulus/response theory.

Stimulus/response theory considers that human behavior is caused by external events. For example, a person stops at a traffic light because it turns red. Control theory, in contrast, is based on the premise that all human behavior is generated by what goes on inside the behaving person. A person stops at a traffic light not because the light turns red, but because that person thinks, "I want to stay alive." All that we get from the outside world is information. We then choose to act on that information in the way we believe is best for us.

In his book, Glasser reviews his experiences interviewing seventh and eighth grade students who were picked at random in a middle school. His purpose was to get them to disclose what school pictures they had (the way they perceived school to be). In asking this question, Glasser was trying to find out if these "pictures" related to the students' need for power. Glasser also asked each student if he or she would like to work together on small teams in their classes, instead of by themselves as they usually worked.

What Did the Researcher Find?

Glasser found that whatever importance students attached to school had little to do with their studies. School was important because they had friends.

They agreed that if any students felt important, it would be class officers and the student council members. But they also made it clear that unless you were popular, you had no chance to get elected, confirming that importance comes through social contact, not academic achievement. In general, the students did not feel important at school or feel they had any power.

In response to the question, would they like to work in learning teams, the students were all both enthusiastic about the idea and disappointed that they had so little teaming in their present classes. There was no doubt that learning teams were needed—to create a satisfying picture in their heads. There was not nearly enough team learning available in their school.

Glasser proceeds to translate control theory into a practical and productive model of team learning with emphasis on helping students enjoy and feel satisfied while engaging in learning. He proposes a three-pronged implementation program:

1. Teach control theory to teachers, who can begin by using it in their personal lives.

2. Implement learning teams and other control theory approaches in the classroom.

3. Teach control theory to students starting in kindergarten.

Students should be taught that they have needs, that they're always trying to satisfy those needs, and that, when they behave well or when they behave badly in the classroom, they are making choices in an attempt to satisfy their needs.

What Are Possible Implications
for School Improvement?

- Classroom instructional characteristics of effective schools successfully structure and appropriately manage cooperative group learning much of the time. Such instruction brings into the classroom the same approach that schools use so successfully in extracurricular activities.

- Understanding control theory is critical both to understanding and to solving the problem of discipline in the schools—the need to empower students.

- In all schools, but especially secondary schools, the thrust is to focus on teaching and learning as the schools' primary mission.

— Michelle Maksimowicz

EFFECTIVE SCHOOLS RESEARCH ABSTRACTS

SAFE AND ORDERLY ENVIRONMENT

CITATION: Allen, James D., "Classroom Management: Students' Perspectives, Goals, and Strategies," *American Educational Research Journal* 23, 3 (Fall 1986): 437-459.

What Did the Researcher Do?

This research paper presents the methods and findings of a field study aimed at understanding high school students' perspectives of classroom management. The author enrolled in four ninth grade classes in a southern California high school and collected data as a participant/observer. He participated in class work, activities, tests, and homework as if he were a student. Although he was initially concerned that his age (30) and his bearded appearance would be barriers to students accepting him as just another student, the literature had suggested that this would not be a problem. That proved to be the case: his "classmates" were neither overly curious or friendly at the beginning of the study. Typically, the other students thought that he had never finished high school and was now trying to finish.

The researcher had earlier explained his purpose to the teachers of the four classes in which he was enrolled and had asked them to treat him as just another student. They cooperated to the point of sending him to the office for a tardy slip when he was late for class and reprimanding him for turning in an incorrect homework assignment.

During class time, he made observational notes and these served as a major source of data. A second data source was provided by interviews with 15 ninth-grade students and a third source of information consisted of interviews with the four teachers.

What Did the Researcher Find?

The researcher attempted to discover the students' "classroom agenda." He discerned that their agenda consists of two major classroom goals and six general strategies that they used in attempting to achieve their goals.

The two major goals of students during class time are to socialize and to pass the course. The goal of socializing involves interactions that usually concern nonacademic matters and are characterized by talking, joking about out-of-class interests, and engaging in playful behavior. The second goal of passing the course is characterized by students engaging in activities that will help them satisfy course requirements. These activities are viewed by students as "work" and include class work, homework, board work, seat work, oral drill work, written work, and worksheets.

With few exceptions, all student behavior in classrooms was directed toward fulfilling these two major goals.

The students used six strategies in attempting to achieve their goals. The first strategy is referred to by the researcher as "figuring out the teacher." It is an effort to find out what the teacher is like, the teacher's limits on socializing, and the requirements for passing the course. Two common tactics in this strategy involve a "wait and see" period, characterized by extreme quiet on the part of students, and testing the teacher to see how far he or she can be pushed regarding limits and requirements.

After the first few days, students used three strategies that directly helped them achieve their goals. The "having fun" strategy was used to socialize and included humor, playing around, and social talking. Most students felt that a teacher's sense of humor contributed positively to the management of the class by promoting a more relaxed and social environment. "Giving the teacher what he wants" was a strategy that students used to complete the requirements necessary for passing the course. This included independently working on assignments, participating in drills and discussion, and studying for tests. Another strategy used by students was "minimizing work." Minimizing work included students helping each other on work assignments and completing assignments at the last moment, often by copying another student's work. Also, students challenged the teacher about the amount and degree of class work, homework, and tests. Having fun, giving the teacher what he wants, and minimizing work were strategies students used during routine classroom events.

Two other strategies, "reducing boredom" and "staying out of trouble," were used when the teacher's agenda conflicted with the students' agenda. They occurred during two critical classroom events. The first occurred when students found the class boring. Reducing boredom was different from having fun, because students focused on trying to change the teacher's work agenda when they found it boring. The students' behavior in this strategy was often aggressive or defiant. Humor used in reducing boredom was sarcastic and demeaning.

The second critical event occurred when the teacher would initiate strict measures to control student socializing. Students would then initiate the strategy "staying out of trouble." This strategy helped them to obtain at least a minimal passing grade in the course. Tactics included attending to class work, terminating talking and play, and changing seats to get away from another student causing trouble.

In classes with low academic demands, students focused on their socializing goal by utilizing "having fun" and "reducing boredom" strategies. In classes with high academic demands, students used the "give the teacher what he wants" strategy in order to pass the course. However, when students were bored by academic work and instructional routines, they engaged in a "minimizing work" strategy in order to create more time to socialize.

For students, a class that allows them to socialize while learning something interesting is the best type of class. Students accept high work demands and instructional routines and even enjoy them in classes where they are allowed to socialize while doing academic tasks.

Classrooms that are managed to develop cooperative student-teacher and student-student relationships tend to be classrooms in which students enjoy learning. Classrooms that are managed and controlled to focus primarily on individual learning activities (nonsocial) do not provide enjoyable learning activities for most students.

What Are Possible Implications for School Improvement?

One of the most frequent phrases found in the effective schools literature describes effective schools as being "orderly without being oppressive." Occasionally, as schools attempt to implement school improvement plans, the emphasis on "orderly" overshadows the notion that effective schools are not rigid, oppressive places for students.

Students see classrooms as places where they can learn what they need to learn to pass the course, but at the same time, they want to be able to socialize. "If a goal of classroom instruction is to foster student learning and a desire to learn, classroom management must not be seen only from a teacher's perspective focused on control and discipline, but also from the student's perspective focused on learning in a sociable environment," the author comments.

This study reinforces the basic assumption that it is possible to have classroom discipline and, at the same time, have a climate that encourages students to enjoy school, their friends, and their studies.

— Robert Eaker and James Huffman

EFFECTIVE SCHOOLS RESEARCH ABSTRACTS

SAFE AND ORDERLY ENVIRONMENT

CITATION: Evertson, Carolyn M., "Managing Classrooms: A Framework for Teachers," Chapter 3 in David Berliner and Barak Rosenshine's *Talks to Teachers*. Random House, New York, NY (1987): 54-74.

What Did the Researcher Do?

One of the enduring tasks of teaching is the orchestration of classroom events so that they serve the curriculum goals of the teacher and the classroom. Evertson recognizes that generally teachers are left on their own to solve the management and organization problems inherent in teaching a large group of students on a daily basis. Teachers have used their own inventiveness to develop ways of creating productive and orderly classrooms, and some teachers have been more effective than others in this endeavor. To better assist more teachers, Evertson and colleagues carefully studied 27 self-contained third-grade classrooms and 51 mathematics and English teachers at the junior high school level. In both settings, the research team conducted interviews and observations before the school year started, at the beginning of the school year, and throughout the year. The primary research question they sought to answer through the analysis of these data was: "Are there principles of management, organization, and group processes that are most effective for beginning the school year, as well as most effective throughout the year?"

What Did the Researcher Find?

The researcher found that teachers who were more effective tended to operate from a framework that functioned well. Other teachers could be taught through inservices to use these principles successfully and create classroom environments with better student engagement, less off-task behavior, and less inappropriate and disruptive behavior.

The author summarizes the principles according to a three-part framework:

1. Planning before the year begins

2. Getting started during the first few weeks of school

3. Maintaining the system throughout the school year

Planning before school begins. Effective classroom managers are very aware of the physical space of the classroom and give careful consideration to how it is best used. Several related guidelines were suggested:

- Students should have a clear view of instructional displays.

- High traffic areas should be kept clear and separated from each other, if possible.

- Attractions that tend to compete with the teacher for student's attention (e.g., a view of the playground) should be minimized.

- General classroom rules should be well thought out before school begins, and they should be thoroughly taught.

- Generally, it is better to have a few guidelines which are clearly stated with supportive rationale. Whenever possible, specific rules should be associated with specific tasks (e.g., turn in homework).

- More effective classroom managers used "warm up" activities to check student learning, provide feedback and correctives, and generally check for understanding.

- Rules and norms for appropriate behavior should have implicit consequences for noncompliance.

Teachers found that rules will be followed if students are clear about the consequences.

In general, effective classroom managers plan their procedures based on the goal of helping students to develop self-control and, ultimately, manage their own behavior.

Implementing the planned management system. Perhaps the most important lesson learned by the researchers was that students' first impressions about their classroom and teachers tend to have a lasting effect on their attitudes and behaviors. To set a positive tone, teachers should plan as follows for the start of school activities each school year:

- Provide students with places to sit, name tags, and a chance to be introduced.

- Provide instruction on how to use the room and its materials.

- Teach rules and procedures, as suggested previously.

- Attend to both the procedures and the course content (at the secondary level).

In summary, the researchers pointed out that time invested in establishing a comprehensive system at the beginning of the year will pay handsome dividends throughout the year.

Maintaining the system throughout the year. The researchers found three domains are critical throughout the year.

- Consistent monitoring of student work and behavior is needed to watch for signs of student confusion. This will help to spot potential behavioral problems, as well as monitor student learning.

- Teachers need to assess the long- and short-term responses to student misbehavior quickly. The general rule is that all inappropriate behavior should be handled promptly to avoid having it continue and spread.

- Celebrations of success and accomplishments are important. Effective classroom celebrations help establish a positive climate and allow students to make positive transitions.

What Are Possible Implications for School Improvement?

The research summarized above has been used to form the basis for a staff development program that has received the approval of the National Diffusion Network. The program is titled "Classroom Organization and Management Program" and includes a series of modules designed to assist teachers with all aspects of their classroom management routines.

A second important implication that may be lost in this research is to remember that individual classroom rules and procedures must build upon, and be consistent with, the school-wide rules and procedures. Therefore, as teachers begin to plan their individual classroom routines, the principal should convene the entire faculty to discuss and, where necessary, change any school rules prior to the opening of school. In addition, teachers and/or the principal should have a plan for explicitly teaching these rules along with the classroom routines.

Before teachers leave in the summer, the faculty should be convened to discuss the events of the previous year. If they wait until the beginning of a school year, problem rules or procedures may be forgotten, and may not reappear until school is again underway, at which time they become more difficult to change.

— Lawrence W. Lezotte

EFFECTIVE SCHOOLS RESEARCH ABSTRACTS

SAFE AND ORDERLY ENVIRONMENT

CITATION: McCollum, Heather, "Instructional Strategies and Classroom Management," *Better Schooling for Children of Poverty: Alternatives to Conventional Wisdom.* U.S. Department of Education, Washington, D.C. (1990): XII-3—XII-24.

What Did the Researcher Do?

This article is based on a review of the research on instructional strategies and approaches to managing classrooms. The review is limited to research that generalizes across subject-matter areas. But it covers two problems that confront all teachers, regardless of the subject matter they teach—instructional strategy and classroom management. The author defines numerous strategies and approaches that are effective for disadvantaged (at-risk) students, only some of which can be covered in this brief abstract.

What Did the Researcher Find?

Grouping. In reviewing the research on grouping, the author found some consensus that tracking has negative effects on the achievement, self-esteem, and educational aspirations of low-ability students. Studies of tracking and within-class grouping show that the slight advantage gained by high-ability students was more than offset by the negative results for middle- and low-achieving students. Group placement tends to be permanent rather than flexible, and students' learning is limited by the kind of instruction they receive in low-ability groups. (pp. XII-6–7)

Structuring participation and communication. Research on verbal participation of students indicated that the ability level of students affects their degree of verbal participation in lessons. Teachers call on high achievers more often and give them a longer time to respond. Teachers are more likely to praise high achievers and to criticize low achievers.

Evidence suggests that the amount of time teachers wait for students to respond is too short and should be increased from an average of one second to somewhere between three and five seconds. Also, teachers often do not communicate clearly as to how students are to participate and respond. (pp. XII-7–8)

Approach to delivery of lessons. The author reviewed studies regarding instructional approaches that may be more effective and found the results inconclusive. Regarding the mastery learning approach, some studies show that the approach does increase the amount of basic skills that are learned, but does not seem to decrease the amount of time required to learn higher-level skills.

Analysis of research on direct instruction suggests that the model does increase the achievement of disadvantaged students in basic skill areas. But it limits the range of curriculum that can be taught and may limit learning of higher-order skills. The author differentiates between "direct instruction" and "active teaching" in her analysis. While "active teaching" involves a large amount of teacher guidance, it allows for more student participation and group involvement, and is suited to a variety of curricular goals. The "active teaching" approach has found far more empirical support among researchers. (p. XII-10)

While exclusive reliance on direct instruction approaches limits the kind of learning that may occur, active teaching of mental processes (cognitive modeling) may have a particular payoff for disadvantaged students. The children from disadvantaged backgrounds should be explicitly taught the content and verbal strategies they need to become part of the dominant culture in the school.

Unlike direct instruction, cooperative and team learning approaches give "a substantial degree of control to students who act as a resource for each other's learning...While...small groups may be complex and difficult to orchestrate (Brophy and Good, 1986), they have been shown to have very positive effects on achievement, particularly for lower-ability students, and on achieving social goals such as intercultural understanding and friendliness in heterogeneous groups (Cohen, 1988)." (p. XII-11)

Low-ability students generally require more mediation in skill learning, but in cooperative learning arrangements, some of the mediation function can be transferred to higher-ability students, who then serve as "substitute teachers."

Structuring academic tasks. The author notes that the teacher is not alone in structuring academic tasks. In subtle ways, students tend to negotiate academic demands with teachers. "Although teachers may be primarily responsible for decisions about what constitutes 'knowledge,' students have almost infinite potential to offer resistance and, thus, determine the pacing of the curriculum and what actually gets accomplished. Often students are more cooperative in tasks that involve rote skills, and they resist higher-order tasks like expository writing." (p. XII-13) Thus, if learning is to occur, the teacher must achieve a delicate balance between challenging students and providing opportunities for success. When manage-ment concerns are paramount, teachers are more likely to reduce academic demands. This may happen more frequently in classes with a high proportion of disadvantaged students.

Facilitating order. Research on classroom management traditionally has focused on disruptive student behavior. But recent research has stressed "preventive" rather than "remedial" approaches to establishing orderly classrooms. Some research has found no differences in the ways that good and poor managers handle classroom disruptions. It appears that the difference lies in the ability of the good managers to prevent classroom management problems through management of instruction and advance planning.

Keeping students engaged in constructive academic activities is a critical element in maintaining good classroom management. The article reports studies showing almost a 99 percent student engagement rate in classes of the most successful teachers, compared with a 25 percent engagement rate in the classes of teachers who were struggling. The author suggests that "some teachers are simply more effective at establishing an orderly environment, regardless of the student composition of the class." (p. XII-21)

Effective classroom managers teach the rules and procedures of the classroom early in the year and consistently monitor compliance with those rules. Good managers organize instruction effectively by communicating objectives and directions clearly, maintaining an appropriate pace and momentum in lessons, and losing little time during transitions. They have more detailed and consistent account-ability systems for students and give clearer descriptions of their evaluation system.

The author comments that the literature reviewed indicates that, "in general, the most effective instructional strategies for all types of students simultaneously increase the amount of student engagement and establish order." She cites instructional strategies for the effective instruction of disadvantaged students. (Brophy, 1986)[1] Some of these are:

- emphasis on academic instruction, along with expectations that students will learn

- more student time spent being taught by teachers

- teachers' enthusiasm in presenting material

- correct answers acknowledged by teachers

- seatwork assignments that are varied and challenging

- individualized instruction for some Chapter 1 students

What Are Possible Implications for School Improvement?

Effective schools are characterized, in part, by effective teaching. This synthesis of effective teaching behaviors has two important implications for those interested in school improvement:

1. What teachers do makes a difference. Some teaching behaviors are clearly more effective than others.

2. Some teaching behaviors are particularly effective with low-achieving students. Obviously, schools attempting to raise student achievement scores must pay specific attention to raising the achievement of this particular group. McCollum's study will make teachers aware of how they can positively affect the achievement of disadvantaged students.

— Robert Eaker and James Huffman

---

[1] Brophy, J., "Research Linking Teacher Behavior to Student Achievement: Potential Implications for Chapter 1 Students," In *Designs for Compensatory Education: Conference Proceedings and Papers.* Research and Evaluation Associates, Washington, D.C., 1986.

Section V

Character

Education

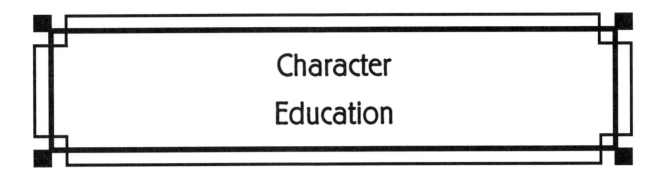

Character Education

"The very profession of teaching calls on us to try to produce not merely good learners, but good people," Alfie Kohn, noted scholar of human behavior and education, tells us.

In recent years, with the decline of the nuclear family and the disturbing trend in youth violence, the schools are now seen as essential in assuming at least some of the family's traditional role of character education.

- Character develops within an environment where there are clear rules of conduct, student ownership of those rules, a supportive environment, and a sense of satisfaction resulting from compliance with those rules.

- Cooperative learning shows promise in bringing about positive changes in behavior, as well as increased knowledge and improved attitudes.

- Individual teachers must act as mentors and models, setting a good example by supporting positive social behavior.

- Students need to be taught specific skills for conflict resolution.

- Parents must be involved as partners with the school in character education, and given specific help on how to reinforce values at home.

- Community leaders, local government, businesses, and the media also need to be involved.

Values rub off on children. If character education is to be effective, it cannot be limited to a course of study in a classroom. Instead, it must pervade the entire building, starting with the principal. A comprehensive approach, making constructive use of the school environment, policies, and practices, is required.

EFFECTIVE SCHOOLS RESEARCH ABSTRACTS

SAFE AND ORDERLY ENVIRONMENT

CITATION: Howe, Harold, "Can Schools Teach Values?" *Teachers College Record* 89, 1 (Fall 1987): 55-68.

What Did the Researcher Do?

Harold Howe, a senior lecturer at Harvard University School of Education and a former teacher, principal, and superintendent, writes about the issue of teaching values in schools. In his study, he reviews his experiences and selected findings on this issue.

He sees schools as facing an ever-increasing responsibility for teaching values to children. He describes the shifting economy and changing family structures in the United States as crucial signals that schools must play an integral part in developing children's characters and in molding the values they will need to lead successful adult lives. Howe sees a triangle of influence upon children's value development: family, religion, and schools.

What Did the Researcher Find?

Families are by far the greatest source of value development for children. Family structure, however, has become increasingly unstable. In impoverished families and one-parent households in which the parent works full-time, the support structure and positive adult role models for children disappear. As the nature of work in today's economy continues to change, bringing more women into the work force, schools will become a more important source of value development for young people.

Schools usually provide two major types of values: a central core of democratic heritage—the ideas of morality, citizenship, and liberty—and commonly shared ethical values, such as integrity and honesty. Schools in the midst of reforms and funding crises often find themselves overburdened with competing interests in terms of their roles in developing morals and values for children. Youth today are increasingly isolated from the adult world and have become somewhat alienated from adult values. In too many instances, schools function as "holding tanks" and "babysitters" in the eyes of both parents and students. Too often the objectives of teaching, learning, and caring are overshadowed by priorities which do not focus on what is best for children.

Reforms which often have close ties to the business community tend to overemphasize achievement scores, course content, and "excellence" more than taking personal interest in seeing that each child has an opportunity to learn in a caring environment which builds constructive attitudes. Unless there is some friendliness, warmth, and respect between teachers and learners, not even the most significant lesson will prove much. The school is partially to blame, however, for failing to recognize the importance of human relationships in promoting students' success.

Howe sees several conflicts in schools which have a negative impact for value development. First, the relationship between families and schools has not been established strongly enough. The greatest problem lies in "bringing together" parents and schools. Once a partnership is built, there is an "endless agenda" for both parents and school to explore jointly, ranging from learning goals to discipline for each individual child.

Second, Howe cites a "hidden curriculum" which underlies the structure of the school, a negative influence which emphasizes conformity. It is responsible for institutionalizing ideas which are dominant in the social structure. But the hidden curriculum fails to leave room for divergent ideas and opposing and alternative cultures in its choice of textbooks, courses excluded from the curriculum, etc. Howe points to sex education as an example of "value instruction" largely left out of the curriculum. Young people consequently lack assistance with a complex matter that is more on their minds than most school subjects.

Third, Howe criticizes the proliferation of competitive values in schools and blames secondary schools for sorting and selecting students instead of providing teaching and learning for all students. After elementary school, where sharing and consideration for others are common lessons, secondary education sets forth another set of priorities. Competition and "getting ahead" are more valued than cooperation and encouragement of learning at individual levels of ability. Humanistic values are often foreshadowed by the mentality of "winning." Schools "push" students toward such goals as scoring high on achievement tests, rather than emphasizing learning for all children.

What Are Possible Implications for School Improvement?

Howe states that the most important factor commonly missing from many school reform programs is the schools' responsibility in establishing the "roots" which enable students to lead successful adult lives. He argues that schools are responsible for pushing negative messages and that youth are inadequate and unsuccessful because two elements—hope and love—are missing. The school must play an important role in putting forth these values into the structure where learning takes place. Reflecting on what we know about changes in the family, changes in the work habits of adults, the relative isolation of youth from the adult world, and the nature and spirit of new demands on schools, one cannot help wondering whether young people are not being shortchanged for both hope and love.

Values rub off on children, if schools have high expectation for students' success and if the student/ teacher relationship is continually enhanced. Any reform must, therefore, include a strong commitment to the integration of values into both the learning climate and the curriculum of the school. Although Howe confirms that using a direct approach to teaching values (i.e. a "Values" course) is not necessarily productive in the long term, the school can reinforce positive values and infuse the "hope and love" approach into the overall structure of the school. School improvement is not brought about simply by increasing achievement scores.

— Molly J. Allen

SAFE AND ORDERLY ENVIRONMENT

CITATION: Hanson, Sandra L. and Alan L. Ginsburg, "Gaining Ground: Values and High School Success," *American Educational Research Journal* 25, 3 (Fall 1988): 334-365.

What Did the Researchers Do?

This article looks at the effect that attitudes and values of students, their parents, and their peers have in the educational achievement process. Using the nationally representative High School and Beyond data from the National Center for Education Statistics (1983), the authors studied the relationship between a wide range of values that stress the idea of responsibility and high school students' test scores, grades, discipline problems, and dropout status. The authors also examined the extent to which student behavior outside of school, such as time spent watching television and doing homework, influenced the relationship between values and high school outcomes. "Our research goes beyond previous research in (a) looking at a broader range of value variables and student outcomes, (b) considering the mechanisms through which values potentially affect school outcomes, and (c) testing the causal sequencing of the values and school outcome variables." (p. 335)

"Values" refers to a set of indicators that are likely to influence whether adolescents will act responsibly with regard to their school achievement and behavior.

A review of the research indicated that values may play an important role in achievement and school behavior processes. The literature was not definitive, however, about the nature and direction of these effects. There were also serious shortcomings in the research reviewed, such as nonprobability samples, outdated data, and lack of important control variables.

Thus, there was a need for systematic values research employing a multivariate design, current data, a probability sample, internal and external controls, and a broad range of values and student outcomes. The data for this research project came from the sophomore cohort of the 1980–1982 High School and Beyond surveys. The base-year data were collected in the spring of 1980 from more than 30,000 tenth-grade students at 1,100 schools. Response rates were 84 percent for the questionnaire and 77 percent for the achievement tests.

The follow-up sample was collected in the spring of 1982. In both the base-year and the follow-up questionnaires, students gave extensive information on a broad range of individual, family, and school characteristics. Achievement tests in reading and mathematics were given to the sophomore groups in 1980 and 1982, including those who dropped out.

What Did the Researchers Find?

Working with a cross-sectional model and using various statistical procedures, including regression coefficients and standardized correlation coefficients, the authors reported the effects of values and other variables on high school outcomes and out-of-school behavior.

High school outcomes. Variables in all three groups—family and individual characteristics; students', parents', and peers' values; and student out-of-school behavior—significantly affect high school outcomes of white students. Values, in particular, play an important role in the processes affecting math and reading scores, grade point average, and discipline problems. Values with the largest influence on the high school outcomes of white students include a student's feeling of control, educational expec-tations, peer values, and parents' educational expectations.

The group of values variables makes a significant contribution to the outcomes of black high school students. Fewer values variables are significant, however, for blacks than for whites because of the smaller sample size and larger sampling error associated with the black sample.

The total effect of the values variables (taken as a whole) on high school outcomes was evaluated and then compared to the total effect of family socioeconomic status (SES). Regression coefficients indicated that, for both races and for all outcomes, the block of values variables has a larger effect on high school success than does the block of variables measuring the SES of the adolescent's family. The effect of values as compared to SES is especially large in the grade point average and discipline equations for blacks and in the discipline equation for whites. Of further interest is that values overall have an effect on the school success of white and black students that is more than twice the size of the effects of SES.

Based on a change model, the researchers found similar effects of the importance of values on both school outcomes and out-of-school behaviors.

For whites, feelings of control, parental concern, and parents' educational expectations significantly affect changes in reading scores. Out-of-school behaviors play not only an important mediating role between values and level of achievement, but also mediate the relationship between values and changes in achievement.

For blacks, there are similar values effects that are consistent with the effects for whites. And for blacks, as for whites, the effects of values are as large as, or larger than, the effects of the family background variables. When the ratio of the values effect to the SES effect is averaged across the two achievement outcomes (reading and math), the values have an effect 44 percent larger than the effect of SES in the white equations and 51 percent larger in the black equation. (p. 360)

Out-of-school behaviors. The group of values variables as a whole indicate a significant effect on all out-of-school behaviors, above and beyond that explained by family and individual background. Values especially influence the amount of time spent doing homework, watching television, and reading. Values with the strongest impact on these behavior variables include students' feeling of control and parents' concern.

What Are Possible Implications for School Improvement?

In light of the widespread and often strident voices proclaiming the decline of American education, this research suggests that students' attitudes and values play a critical role in raising the quality of American education. The findings in this study support the hypothesis that when students, their parents, and their peers believe in values and accompanying behaviors that stress responsibility, those students have a better chance of achieving success in high school. "If values of students, parents, and peers indeed play an important role in high schoolers' achievement and behavior by affecting the effort of the student, as our research suggests, there may be cause for considerable optimism. Values (and the efforts they spur) may be more conducive to change and hence may allow more equality of opportunity than would be the case if family socioeconomic status and/or students' innate ability were the only determinants of school achievement." (p. 361)

— Frank X. Ferris

EFFECTIVE SCHOOLS RESEARCH ABSTRACTS

SAFE AND ORDERLY ENVIRONMENT

CITATION: Kohn, Alfie, "Teaching Children to Care," *Phi Delta Kappan* 72, 7 (March 1991): 496-506.

What Did the Researcher Do?

Over 50 years ago, the noted philosopher Martin Buber told a group of teachers, "Education worthy of the name is essentially education of character." This statement can be translated into specific actions of teachers and administrators, says Kohn. He believes that "the very profession of teaching calls on us to try to produce not merely good learners, but good people." (p. 497)

Disturbed by a pervasive attitude that "students are graduated who think that being smart means looking out for number one," Kohn, a scholar of human behavior and education, develops three arguments which focus on helping children become caring adults: first, something can be done; second, educators should do something; and third, psychological research, common sense, and the results of a significant pilot project offer specific suggestions to educators. (p. 498)

What Did the Researcher Find?

"Much of what takes place in a classroom...emerges from a set of assumptions about the nature of human nature," says Kohn. (p. 498) This becomes apparent when we attempt to influence children's behavior. Our goal is to curb or "discipline" negative behaviors, rather than promote positive ones.

The author asserts that, in this culture, we believe our darker side is more pervasive. We seem to assume that people are naturally and primarily selfish and will act otherwise only if they are coerced into doing so and are carefully monitored. Kohn cites recent mental health research which shows that very young children are aware of and respond to the needs of others. (p. 498) He believes that schools have not been inclined to guide children toward caring about, empathizing with, and helping other people, suggesting that parents, teachers, and others have three specific objections to classroom programs to strengthen children's prosocial development. The first objection

has to do with the teaching of values, which, they say, should not be on the agenda of a public institution. But everything the teacher says, and does, her tone of voice, choice of lesson, etc., are "saturated in values, regardless of whether those values are transparent to the teacher." (p. 499) While no one disagrees that moral concerns and social skills ought to be taught at home, Kohn points out that "someone to model altruism, opportunities to practice caring for others, and so forth—is not to be found in all homes. The school may need to provide what some children will not otherwise get... there is no conceivable danger in providing these values in both [school and home]." (p. 499)

A second objection is the fear that children taught to care for others will be "unable to look out for themselves when they are released into a heartless society." (p. 499) Kohn cites research which shows that those who look out for number one are actually at a greater disadvantage in any society than those who are skilled at working with others.

A third objection to teaching children to be caring individuals is that it takes time from academics. Again, Kohn claims that there is no evidence to suggest that learning experiences that help to create prosocial children are mutually exclusive with academic achievement. He notes that cooperative learning, an important element in a prosocial classroom, enhances achievement, regardless of subject matter or age level.

Kohn expresses the belief that the absence of behavior problems in a classroom is not an invitation to then get on with the "business at hand"—academic learning. He believes that "behavioral and social issues, values and character, are very much part of the business at hand," and discusses in ascending order four approaches to changing behaviors and attitudes: (p. 500)

1. **Punishing.** Punishment focuses attention on the punishment itself and not on the intended lesson.

"The one who punishes becomes transformed in the child's eyes as a rule-enforcer who is best avoided." (p. 500)

2. **Bribing.** The author cites research by Robert Sternberg and others which concluded that extrinsic motivators tend to undermine creativity as well as intrinsic motivation. "Gold stars, smiley faces… certificates…are [all] artificial attempts to manipulate behavior that offer children no reason to continue acting in the desired way when there is no longer any goody to be gained." (p. 500)

Kohn cites research over the past 15 years which tends to have similar findings: "An education based on rewards leads the child to ask, 'What am I supposed to do, and what will I get for doing it?'"(pp. 500–502)

3. **Encouraging commitment to values.** The author believes that a student manipulated by currently fashionable behavioral techniques is unlikely to get and internalize the values underlying desired behaviors. "The teacher ought to be guided less by the need to maintain control over the classroom than by the long-term objective of helping students act responsibly because they understand it is right to do so…When values have been internalized by the child, the question becomes 'What kind of person do I want to be?'"(pp. 501–502)

4. **Encouraging the group's commitment to values.** Kohn advocates this approach because it teaches and helps students internalize responsibility and helpfulness within a community of people rather than in a vacuum. He sees advantages in increased student interactions through the process of cooperative learning. "Cooperation is an essentially humanizing experience that predisposes participants to take a benevolent view of others…teachers can move the idea of discipline not only away from punishments and rewards…but rather to bring in…children so that they can play a role in making decisions about how their classroom is to be run and why." (p. 504)

He cites a pilot project of a school district in California where a Child Development Program (CDP) has been designed to help children become more caring and responsible. CDP is a long-term, comprehensive, school-based project in prosocial education in the San Ramon Valley Unified School District, which was started in 1982. It focused on a group of kindergarten children (now in junior high) and compared their attitudes, behavior, and achievement to a control group. The experimental group participated in a program which presented:

- a version of cooperative learning that does not rely on grades or other extrinsic motivators.

- the use of a literature-based reading program that stimulates discussion about values and offers examples of empathy and caring as it develops verbal skills.

- an approach to classroom management in which the emphasis is on developing intrinsic motivation to participate productively and prosocially.

- a variety of other features, such as pairing children of different ages to work together, community service projects to develop responsibility, giving periodic homework assignments to be done with parents, and holding school-wide activities for families.

Results of this program have already shown positive effects. Children who participated in CDP are showing evidence of a greater number of prosocial behaviors, are more likely to understand hypothetical conflict situations, will speak up in discussions, and are outscoring others on a measure of higher-order reading comprehension.

What Are Possible Implications for School Improvement?

The author states that it is both realistic and valuable to attend to what students learn in the classroom about getting along with their peers. Lezotte, in his recently published monograph, *Correlates of Effective Schools: The First and Second Generation*, reinforces Kohn's statement in emphasizing the necessity for schools to move beyond the first correlate standards.

Second generation correlates emphasize the necessity for the creation of schools where students help one another, says Lezotte. In such schools, teachers have high expectations for self, as well as students. School missions will emphasize "learning" rather than "teaching," and the focus will be on self-disciplined, socially responsible students. Schools, parents, and the community will form an authentic partnership, and the principal will become a leader of leaders rather than a leader of followers.

— Barbara C. Jacoby

CITATION: Leming, James S., "In Search of Effective Character Education," *Educational Leadership* 51, 3 (November 1993): 63-71.

What Did the Researcher Do?

"The current revival of interest in character education, if it is to succeed, will have to successfully address the question of the assessment of program effectiveness," writes the researcher. "A body of research exists related to the topic of educating for character that can, if utilized and expanded, inform practice and assist in the development of effective programs." (p. 63) In this article, he reviews the character education movement in the early years of the century. He also surveys current values education activities, examining many research and evaluation efforts to identify effective aspects of these programs.

Character education became a major preoccupation in this country in response to the social upheavals caused by "increasing industrialization and urbanization, the continuing tide of immigration, World War I, the Bolshevik Revolution, and the spirit of the Roaring '20s...[when] social stability was [perceived as] being threatened and...moral standards needed to be strengthened." (p. 63) A Children's Morality Code was developed in 1917, which emphasized "ten laws of right living" (e.g., kindness, duty, reliability, truth), to be integrated into all aspects of school life and promoted by special student clubs. A decade later, a Character Education Inquiry into the schools' role in the development of character regretfully concluded: "The mere urging of honest behavior by teachers or the discussion of standards and ideals of honesty...has no necessary relation to conduct...the prevailing ways of inculcating ideals probably do little good and do some harm." (quoted on p. 64) A renewed interest in character education began in 1966 with the publication of Lawrence Kohlberg's theories of moral reasoning. At about the same time, values clarification, with its seven-step process for examining and clarifying values, became a popular activity in the schools.

Leming's survey of the literature on these approaches leads him to conclude that the research base for "the morals and values education curriculums of this period offers little assistance in planning for character education where changes in student behavior is a central objective." (p. 65)

During the past 30 years, sex and drug education programs, though not directly related to moral education, have focused on character-related student behavior. Numerous reviews of sex education programs have concluded that they increase student knowledge, and help students become more tolerant of the sexual practices of others, but do not result in significant changes in values or sexual behavior. (p. 65) Drug education has moved from the scare tactics of the 1960s, through the emphasis in the 1970s on personal skills, problem solving, and decision making, to today's "social influences" strategy, which helps students develop skills to resist peer pressure to use drugs. One such program, the Midwestern Prevention Project, has been implemented in 15 communities. By the second year of what is to be a six-year program, use of all three target drugs (tobacco, alcohol, and marijuana) was declining.

Leming also reviews a number of school-based research projects investigating the relationship between school atmosphere and student behavior. He notes that cooperative learning environments have "resulted in impressive student achievement and positive social values and behavior." (p. 66) The "just community approach," developed by Kohlberg and his associates, emphasizes collectively derived social norms rather than individual values as a goal of moral education.

A 1978 study described the Cluster School in Brookline, Massachusetts, where race relations, stealing, drug usage, and absenteeism constituted four problematic areas in the life of the school. "Through a process of collective deliberation, students and teachers proposed and agreed on norms for behavior. The group then enforced compliance. Because this approach harnessed strong peer pressure...students eventually modified antisocial behavior" in three of the above areas, but not in the case of drug usage, "because students did not share the teachers' perception that such a norm was needed." (p. 66)

What Did the Researcher Find?

The present research base is "small, disparate, and inconsistent," observes Leming. (p. 69) He says that character formation or changes in behavior as a result of character education programs are not easily achieved. The researchers for the Character Education Inquiry in 1930 documented many incidents of deceit, which appeared to be unaffected either by character education curriculum in the classroom or by membership in organizations that purported to teach honesty and honest behavior.

Likewise, contemporary researchers have found that didactic methods are unlikely to have significant or long-term effects on character. Many of the sex and drug education programs reviewed succeeded in providing the students with information about the subjects, but did not result in significant changes in values, sexual behavior, or drug use. Students' increased ability to reason about moral issues does not result in changes in conduct. Research conducted on the values clarification theory and practice show minimal significant impact on such variables as values thinking, self-concept, dogmatism, or value-related behavior. Furthermore, a majority of character education programs have been implemented in elementary schools, while the problematic, antisocial behaviors occur primarily during the adolescent years.

Character develops within a social environment where there are clear rules of conduct, student ownership of those rules, a supportive environment, and satisfaction resulting from complying with the norms of the environment shape behavior. "Value-based sex education that involves schools, parents, and the community in a common effort to encourage responsible sexual behavior appears to have some potential for changing adolescent attitudes and sexual behavior." (p. 65) But the small number of evaluations of such programs causes Leming to warn against drawing generalizations from the data.

The programs which emphasize improvement of school environment, including cooperative learning and collective efforts by teachers and students to develop norms for student conduct, show promise of bringing about changes in behavior in addition to increased knowledge and improved attitudes. Reviews of the extensive literature on this topic have found that in addition to increasing academic achievement, students learned to get along better with students of other races and ethnic groups and were more likely to engage in prosocial behavior.

Much of the evaluation of values programs has been based on anecdotal evidence, opinions, and observations by teachers and parents rather than scientifically based studies, using experimental design and controlled comparisons.

What Are Possible Implications for School Improvement?

The theory and practice of character education are still in the early stages. Leming's article emphasizes that the introduction of curriculum materials on values into the classroom is insufficient to bring about changes in student conduct and behavior. Educators seeking to design effective programs must look beyond the pedagogical or rhetorical aspects of values education to a more ecological approach, which includes a change in school climate and involvement of students in developing and accepting norms which may then influence behavioral changes. He proposes three levels of development related to the formation of character:

- Rules are external to the child; conformity is gained through discipline and self-interest.

- Rules are determined by social groups; children comply to gain acceptance within the group.

- Rules are developed and interpreted in terms of self-chosen principles.

These levels might guide the design of programs, from elementary grades, with clear rules in an orderly school environment, through middle grades, with cooperative learning methods and just community environments, up to high school where students have developed the capacity for moral reasoning.

Those involved in designing and implementing character education programs need to give serious thought to including a plan for evaluation. We need to learn which factors and program elements are effective in helping our children grow into adults with a capacity for principled, moral reasoning.

— Nancy Berla

EFFECTIVE SCHOOLS RESEARCH ABSTRACTS

SAFE AND ORDERLY ENVIRONMENT

CITATION: Lickona, Thomas, "The Return of Character Education," *Educational Leadership* 51, 3 (November 1993): 6-11.

What Did the Researcher Do?

Why did support for character education in the schools decline during much of this century? What recent trends have focused new attention on the school's role in teaching values? What practices in the classroom can be instituted to exemplify and enhance character development?

In this article, Lickona looks at several philosophical trends during much of the 20th century, which have contributed to the declining interest in character education in the schools. He then identifies and discusses three factors related to a new groundswell of interest in teaching values. He offers some examples of ongoing efforts to support the resurgence in character education. He asserts that the schools cannot be ethical bystanders and suggests many concrete actions for school personnel to consider.

The author believes that the renewed interest in character education today follows earlier decades when morality "was relativized and privatized" and personal value judgments were not considered proper subjects for a public school curriculum. (p. 6) This was reinforced by the personalism of the 1960s, which emphasized individual rights and the rapidly intensifying pluralism and secularism of American society that posed the question: "Whose values should we teach?"

However, in recent years, with the decline of the family and its role in teaching values to children, the schools are now seen as essential in assuming some of the family's traditional roles of nurturing and character education. This has become all the more urgent in view of recent troubling trends in youth character—violence, dishonesty, bigotry, and self-centeredness. Such trends may be the result of disintegrating families, peer group pressures, and the emphasis on sex, violence, and materialism in the mass media.

But, meanwhile, we are seeing "a recovery of shared, objectively important ethical values," says Lickona. "We are recovering the wisdom that we do share a basic morality, essential for our survival; that adults must teach the young, directly and indirectly, such values as respect, responsibility, trustworthiness, fairness, caring, and civic virtue...Such values affirm our human dignity, promote the good of the individual and the common good, and protect our human rights." (p. 9)

Lickona discusses three examples of the resurgence of character education in the l990s:

- The Aspen Declaration on Character Education, setting forth eight principles of character education. It was prepared by a group of 30 educational leaders, convened by the Josephson Institute of Ethics in July 1992.

- The Character Education Partnership, established in March 1993 under the sponsorship of the Association for Supervision and Curriculum Development (ASCD). It includes representatives from business, labor, government, youth, parents, and religious groups committed to putting character development at the top of the nation's educational agenda.

- A spate of books on the subject in the last two years, as well as a new periodical, the *Journal of Character Education*.

What Did the Researcher Find?

The author contends that successful character education must be grounded in a comprehensive and compelling theory of what good character is, taking into account cognitive, affective, and behavioral aspects of morality. "Schools must help children understand the core values, adopt or commit to them, and then act upon them in their own lives." (p. 9)

The cognitive side of character involves awareness, knowledge, reasoning, and decision making. The affective or emotional aspect includes conscience, self-respect, empathy, self-control, and humility. Moral action requires such additional skills as listening, communicating, cooperating, and "moral habit," the disposition to respond ethically to problematic situations.

Lickona suggests that administrators and teachers examine their practices and policies to ensure that the school climate and classroom environment are supportive of the values espoused by any character education effort. Schools need "to maximize their moral clout, make a lasting difference in students' character, and engage and develop all three parts of character (knowing, feeling, and behavior)... [schools] need a comprehensive, holistic approach... [This means] asking, Do present school practices support, neglect, or contradict the school's professed values and character education aims?" (p. 10) This requires that individual teachers in classrooms will:

- Act as caregivers, models, and mentors, setting a good example by supporting positive social behavior;

- Create a democratic classroom environment, which involves students in decision making and in taking responsibility for a healthy and positive school climate;

- Use cooperative learning to develop students' appreciation of others;

- Teach conflict resolution, so that students learn skills to solve conflicts fairly and without force;

- Treat students with love and respect, helping them to respect and care about one another;

- Practice moral discipline, "using the creation and enforcement of rules as opportunities to foster moral reasoning, voluntary compliance with rules, and a respect for others." (p. 10)

At the school level, efforts can be made to provide opportunities for students in every grade to perform school and community service. The development of a "schoolwide ethos" can be accomplished through leadership of the principal, meaningful student government, and a sense of community that supports and enhances the values taught in the classroom.

The school can involve parents as partners in this endeavor, informing them of the key role they play in developing the moral character of their children, and giving parents specific suggestions of how to reinforce values at home. Community leaders, businesses, churches, local government, and the media can be called upon to help with an initiative to support core ethical values.

What Are Possible Implications for School Improvement?

Lickona concludes that if character education is to be effective in the schools, it cannot be limited to a course of study in the classroom. If character education is to be effective in influencing students in cognitive, emotional, and behavioral ways, the school must make a commitment which goes beyond rhetoric or special curriculum offered in the classroom. "Especially at the building level, it is absolutely essential to have moral leadership that sets, models, and consistently enforces high standards of respect and responsibility. Without a positive schoolwide ethos, teachers will feel demoralized in their individual efforts to teach good values." (p. 11)

A holistic, comprehensive approach making constructive use of the school environment, policies, and practices is required. The author concludes: "As we close out a turbulent century and ready our schools for the next, educating for character is a moral imperative if we care about the future of our society and our children." (p. 11)

— Nancy Berla